An impressive overview of the many things which needs to happen, and best practices for making them happen. Runs the gamut for complete decision-making best practices, from getting and analysing the data, to creating the right culture, people, processes and technology

—**Harphajan Singh**, Head Of Analytics, Prudential Assurance Company Singapore

"James has been at the forefront of decision management techniques for years. This book updates James' proven decision management fundamentals to account for today's world of artificial intelligence and ever broader need for automated decisions. Anyone trying to automate and embed analytics to support decisions should read this book."

—**Bill Franks**, Chief Analytics Officer, International Institute For Analytics, speaker, and author

"An absolute masterclass in analytics from one of the great masters himself. Nothing but solid knowledge, sage advice, and great examples without an ounce of hyperbole or fluff. This book contains just about anything you need to know as business professional to help your organization thrive in the digital age."

—**Doug Laney**, Principal Data Strategist with Caserta, and best-selling author of 'Infonomics'.

"This book elegantly ties modern artificial intelligence concepts to the field of decision management and is grounded in real pragmatic techniques for enterprises to deliver value from AI."

—**Sean Naismith**, VP Decision Services Center of Excellence, TransUnion

"Technology inflection points come once in a generation and Artificial Intelligence combined with actionable business rules makes the present moment as exciting as we've seen in decades. James Taylor presents a guide for beginners and experts alike to understand the practical application of AI with Decision Management. By utilizing one of the most logical linkage points that exist today, that is the marriage of AI with the executable business logic that is inherent in codified work running the world's businesses, Digital Decisioning is a must-read for business and technical leaders who want to operationalize AI, today."

—**Kramer Reeves**, Director, Global Marketing IBM Automation

"James Taylor will transform your approach to Decision Management. The book provides a holistic view of how to operationalize decisions within an organization."

—**Avinash Vaidya**, Business Technology Leader, Franklin Templeton

"This book sets a new milestone in the development of Decision Management. As organisations struggle to reap the results from Artificial Intelligence, this book is a must for these organisations to make the next step in Automated Decisioning. It clearly outlines how to discover and model Digital Decisions, build them and deploy them. James outlines ways to monitor the effects of the Digitized Decisions in real-life operations in order to maximise the business impact. This book bridges the field of Business Analysis and Data Science and gives guidance to the enablers for Digital Decisioning. A must-read book."

—**Peter Kalmijn**, thought-leader EDM and AI, Atos

"Do you wonder what all this fuss around AI, Machine Learning, Big Data, Business Rules, etc. is about from a practical business perspective? Then this book is a must for you! I wondered myself and reading this book clarified many things. It boils down to fusing AI, business rules, and optimization into digital decisioning to manage and automatically take business decisions in processes and workflows. The author uses his extensive knowledge and experience from many different real-world projects to show and explain this integration and why it is so important in today's business world. I highly recommend this book to anyone who is interested in AI, BR, ML, etc. with a business focus and wants to know how it all goes together to produce real business value."

—**Odd Steen**, Associate Professor of Information Systems, Department of Informatics, Lund University, Sweden

"As a practitioner, this is the most concise, compelling and easy to read description of Digital Decisioning that I've seen. It makes a strong case that the most effective means of leveraging AI and machine learning in business applications is by Digital Decisioning. Updated from James's earlier definitive text on Decision Management, this is essential reading for COOs looking to rigorously improve automation through AI."

—**Dr Jan Purchase**, Director Machine Learning and Decision Management, Lux Magi Ltd

"Historically, organizations have codified their best practices in rules. Now they are hungry to take advantage of the possibilities of AI to leverage the wealth of information in their historical data and take even better decisions. They are struggling to do so. James Taylor makes it clear how to succeed: By combining business rules and machine learning in a single digital decisioning framework. With clear explanations and examples based on years of practice, this book lays out what can be accomplished with digital decisioning platforms - and how to go about it successfully."

— **Harley Davis**, VP, Automation Intelligence/France Lab, IBM

"With his new book about Digital Decisioning James Taylor manages to again highlight the importance of decisions and this time with the integration of Artificial Intelligence. He clearly explains why decisions play a crucial role in AI insights into immediate business value. Like in his previous books he shares his enormous expertise by giving countless tips and warnings. And he makes us realize that digital decisioning is taking place now and no longer a future development."

—**Marwim van Overschot**, Senior Business Consultant Atos BTN

"When it comes to describing the power of Decision Management and the use of digital decisioning technologies to automate business interactions, no one has a better grasp of the capabilities than James. One of the biggest marketing challenges we face is figuring out ways to describe the analytic techniques, best practices, and implementation options that uniquely align the technologies to different industries and use cases. James has found a way to break down the technical and provide the most straight forward way to communicate the power of these approaches in a manner we can all understand"

—**Benjamin Baer**, Vice President, Product Marketing, FICO

"James Taylor is a master at extracting complex decisions from people and systems in an organization. This book provides a wealth of practical guidance and real-world examples for getting business value at scale out of everything from the knowledge in your experts' heads to new opportunities in modern artificial intelligence."

—**Tim Gorton**, Principal Architect"

"Shortening the cycle from insights-to-action is the key imperative businesses face in this always-on, hyper-personalized, digital economy where consumers are increasingly demanding that organizations strike the balance between personalization and privacy, customer experience and security. Digital decisioning will enable your business to move faster, build competitive advantage and create awesome customer experiences. A successful program requires your organization to go all-in. This isn't just an IT project. This is a business transformation initiative, and it's worth it! "

—**Melanie Zimmerman**, Senior Vice President, Global Solutions, TransUnion.

"We are early in using AI in the decision cycle for signal/pattern recognition, understanding data/decisions in multiple contexts, assisting to select the decision models/algorithms, take appropriate actions within the guard rails of goals and constraints, and learning from the decision process to become better decision-makers over time. While there are inherent risks in allowing AI to do all this in an unsupervised manner, having AI assist in decision management is the prudent and successful way today. This book nicely ties the theory of decision management with real-world examples where organizations can make traction today leading them into a better decision management process in the future."

—**Jim Sinur**, Former VP and Distinguished Analyst, Gartner Group; Now Independent Analyst

Companion Book

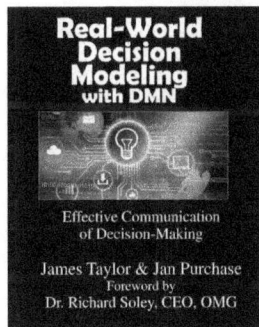

Real-World Decision Modeling with DMN

Effective Communication of Decision-Making

James Taylor & Jan Purchase
Foreword by
Dr. Richard Soley, CEO, OMG

Publisher's Cataloging-in-Publication Data

James Taylor
Digital Decisioning/ James Taylor, - 2nd ed.
 p. cm.

ISBN 10: 0-929652-64-9 ISBN 13: 978-0-929652-64-1
(paperback: alk. paper)

1. Decision Management 2. Digital Decisioning 3. Machine Learning 4. Artificial
Intelligence 5. Predictive Analytics. 6. Business Rules. I. Taylor, James.

HD58.87.S548 2013	2013947326
658.4'063–dc21	CIP

Published by JTonEDM Press

4123 Briarwood Way
Palo Alto, CA 94306 USA

Company and product names mentioned herein are the trademarks or
registered trademarks of their respective owners.

With grateful thanks to the memory of Peter Fingar, founder of
Meghan-Kiffer Press, who originally published this book and who died
March 29, 2022.

Printed in the United States of America.   SAN 249-7980

Digital Decisioning

Using Decision Management to Deliver Business Impact from Artificial Intelligence

James Taylor

JTonEDM Press

Palo Alto, California, USA, jtonedm.com/books

Table of Contents

For Amalia Rose, on her birth

Foreword by Tom Davenport

James Taylor has been a steadfast advocate—the most consistent and prominent one I know of—for the idea of "decision management." That concept—a systematic approach to improving decisions using technology--was the focus of the first edition of this book, and now he has revised it to incorporate the new developments in AI. "Digital decisioning" is an interesting term, and I am sure it is far superior to analog decisioning. More to the point, it suggests that organizations that are serious about decision-making will increasingly model and enable their decisions with sophisticated digital technologies.

I would certainly agree with the author's key argument for the new edition that AI brings new dimensions to decision-making. The primary focus of the decision management movement was rule-based systems, which as Taylor points out were once the primary technology behind the AI of the 1980s and 90s. Contemporary AI is mostly (but not completely) based on statistical machine learning, which has some capabilities that rules do not. It can take vast amounts of data into account, it fosters a probabilistic view of the world (which I believe tends to be the most accurate way to view most decisions), and it can involve many different models that can enable a highly granular view of business phenomena.

But the ideas from the old book—and some of that content is in this one as well—should definitely not be abandoned. I assisted in designing and analyzing one survey a couple of years ago with Deloitte revealing that rules are definitely not dead; 49% of large, AI-aware US companies were using them. Rules have some advantages over machine learning; they are more interpretable and transparent, require less data to develop, are amenable to causal explanations, and in many cases can be modified even by nontechnical users. Some AI experts, such as Gary Marcus of New York University, have argued that we need to return to interpretable and causal systems like rules if we are going to make long-term progress with AI.

Of course, as Taylor points out in Chapter 5, these digital systems will not automate all decisions. If a decision is made only once or rarely, it is unlikely to be suited to digitization. There won't be enough data to draw on, and it may not be economical to build a system to support that kind of decision. Very important digital decisions—particularly the probabilistic ones based on machine learning—will probably need to be reviewed by a human decision-maker.

What that leaves for AI and automation is frequent, tactical decisions that benefit from data and modeling. As Taylor's many examples suggest, there is no shortage of that type of decision in firms today: what price to charge for products and services, what offers to make to customers, what inventory levels to maintain, whether to approve a credit transaction, etc. Companies that make those decisions with the tools and methods described in this book are likely to make them faster and more accurately than those who don't. That's a pretty well-established finding in virtually every area of human endeavor—from business to sports to healthcare to entertainment.

The other good news is that many of the processes for creating and maintaining a digital decision environment—at least those involving machine learning—are being automated. "Automated machine learning" (autoML)) tools are increasingly available from a variety of vendors. They automate such parts of the process as data preparation, feature engineering, algorithm testing, model fitting, model deployment, and even generation of explanations of how the model works. In addition to autoML for model creation, firms are developing "MLOps" tools that automate model management, monitoring, and continuous refitting tasks. These tools can dramatically accelerate the productivity of data scientists, or enable quantitatively-oriented business analysts—"citizen data scientists"—to do work that once required data science skills. Many firms using these tools want to achieve both objectives.

But even automating the creation and management of digital decisions doesn't take humans out of the picture. As Taylor points out, any use of these tools demands that organizations "begin with the decision in mind." That decision needs to be framed by humans—what are we trying to decide, what are the possible outcomes, how will the decision be deployed within the organization, what data might be relevant to it, and so forth. Human decision-makers need to understand how automated decision systems work so that they can decide whether they are relevant to a decision—either at the beginning of creating a digital decision, or if it appears that the world has changed and that digital process is no longer a good representation of it. Systems can hint that decisions aren't as effective as they once were, but it's up to human managers to decide what to do about that.

All of this work with digital decisions also demands that human executives take a new decision-oriented focus on their business. They need to understand what the important, repetitive, and data-based decisions are within their organizations. They won't be able to automate them all at once, so they'll have to create some priorities among decisions. They will have to continuously monitor how automated decision systems are working; there is no faster way to lose money than to be running your business with bad automated decision systems. They need to make wise decisions about what decisions not to automate. In some ways, these digital decisions place an even greater burden on decision-makers than they carried in the past; they need to understand not only the decisions that need to be automated, but how they are automated and how the technology, logic, data and statistics combine to make a good decision.

Large organizations have always involved thousands of daily decisions, many of which were made badly. James Taylor's books—both the previous version and this one—introduce a radically different approach to decision-making that can radically improve organizational performance. Technology and data are creating the supply for this approach, and the complexity of modern business is creating the demand. It won't be easy to embrace digital decisioning, but it will certainly be rewarding.

Thomas H. Davenport
Distinguished Professor, Babson College and Fellow, MIT Initiative on the Digital Economy

Foreword by Eric Siegel

For a rocket scientist, the math isn't the hardest part. What's hard is being so often misunderstood.

The same goes for data scientists, who time and again lack the support needed to successfully launch the fruits of their brilliant labor into action. These math heads have got to integrate into the organization as a whole, lest they vanish into the obscurities of their analysis. Their isolation is an enemy to their usefulness.

After all, the most wicked and pervasive pitfall of predictive analytics is organizational in nature, not technical: Predictive models often fail to launch. They're never deployed to drive decisions. This is ultimately a management error. We must pursue the business of machine learning only so that it delivers the business value of machine learning.

Here's how the delivery of that value works. Operational decisions need prediction. Prediction requires machine learning. And machine learning requires data. Reversing that into sequential order, we have data, we give it to machine learning, it makes models that predict, and we use the predictions to more effectively drive millions of operational decisions. With this in place, we improve all the large-scale organizational functions that make the world go 'round.

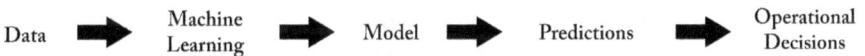

Data ➡ Machine Learning ➡ Model ➡ Predictions ➡ Operational Decisions

The part on the far right, the predictive model's intended operationalization – aka, its deployment or implementation – guides the entire machine learning project. How the model will ultimately be used is the carrot at the end of the stick. It keeps the project moving in the right direction from the get-go.

In a nutshell, we must steer the project towards the intersection of two sets:

Conceivable prediction goals that would be valuable

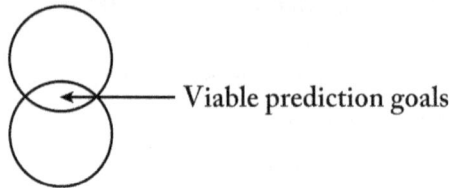

Viable prediction goals

Behaviors that can be analytically predicted

On the top, the range of conceivable prediction goals that would be valuable for digital decisioning is limited only by the imagination of your operations and marketing staff. Prediction goals could be any of a range of behaviors and outcomes, such as which customer will buy or which transaction is likely to be fraudulent. The problem is, some of these ideas aren't doable from an analytical standpoint.

On the bottom, there are many things that could be analytically predicted. So long as there are enough examples in the data, machine learning can generate a predictive model that puts future odds on individual cases. The problem is, many such ideas that sound appealing in the lab would never actually be used, never operationally deployed. Your team may create an elegant, effective predictive model, but that doesn't mean the business is ready to act upon it to drive decisions. All too often, lack of management buy-in or unforeseen business constraints preclude model deployment.

A shrewd business perspective steers clear of this pitfall and navigates to a viable prediction goal within the intersection of these two sets – one that's both achievable and useable. The analytics and number crunching alone do not determine what to actually do with a model's predictions – only business acumen can dictate how to best deploy a model. For example, for targeting a marketing campaign, a predictive model provides a range of options and trade-offs. Such a model could empower you to market to a group of, say, 100,000 customers with a four times greater likelihood of making a purchase – or, alternatively, to a group twice as large but with only three times the likelihood. You've got to choose between these options based on business considerations such as profit and market penetration.

That's where this book comes in. Author James Taylor is the longstanding thought leader in machine learning operationalization – the deployment of predictive models to drive business decisions. He and his firm bridge what is often a wide gulf between business leaders on one side and hands-on analytics practitioners on the other. For many years, James has also brought his insight to Predictive Analytics World, the conference series I founded, where he serves as the co-chair of the operationalization track on machine learning deployment, as well as the instructor of the event's training workshop on this topic.

This comprehensive book guides you to leverage the potential of machine learning. It delivers the business-level finesse needed to ensure predictive models are operationalization-ready. It lays the groundwork and sets the standard. It's a great place to start... and to finish.

Eric Siegel, Ph.D.
Founder, the Predictive Analytics World and Deep Learning World conference series. Author, Predictive Analytics: The Power to Predict Who Will Click, Buy, Lie, or Die

Preface

There is an artificial intelligence (AI) revolution underway as companies adopt predictive analytics, machine learning and a broad range of AI algorithms across their business. Increasingly it is AI, not people, that will make the decisions that matter to an organization. This revolution is being driven by better algorithms, more powerful computers, cloud computing and the explosive growth in digital data.

The hype and breathless boosterism of the technology industry put managers and executives under enormous pressure to use AI to run their companies more effectively.

They're not sure how to do this.

They're a little "afraid" of the math and the complexity.

They're worried that their people will lose their jobs.

Most of all, they're afraid of losing control and becoming the victims of this new AI economy rather than the beneficiaries.

Digital Decisioning unlocks the business value of AI. Just as companies have digitized their data and their processes, they must now digitize their decisions. Information systems must be developed to use AI to decide on your behalf. The scale of data and the complexity of analysis demands nothing less.

The potential value of decision-making AI is great, but so is the scale of the problem. Digital Decisioning is the way forward.

James Taylor, October 2019
CEO, Decision Management Solutions
james@decisionmanagementsolutions.com

A Note on the Second Edition

In 2011 I published a book called Decision Management Systems: A Practical Guide to Using Business Rules and Predictive Analytics. Despite the new name, this is the second edition of that book.

The biggest changes are the name and the first few chapters in this edition. There is still no unanimity on the right name for the result of applying the described approach but Digital Decisioning seems to me to be the most evocative. It ties to digital business and digital transformation while focusing on the core outcome of applying the approach – digitized, automated decisions.

When I wrote Decision Management Systems, the idea that an organization might build systems to automate decisions and use its data to do so effectively was novel enough that several chapters had to be devoted to setting up the value of doing so. No longer. Now it is taken for granted that organizations will use data, machine learning, advanced analytics and artificial intelligence to drive automated responses. Future success, even survival, is widely understood to rely on their ability to do this.

Decision Management remains the name we use for the approach. Chapter 3 remains the same, outlining the key principles of systems developed this way. Chapters 4 through 7 describe the Decision Management approach in detail and represent the core of the book. Experience with modeling and automating thousands of decisions has led to some refinements so that the advice in these chapters better represents how we actually deliver Digital Decisioning. They have also been updated to reflect new terminology around machine learning and artificial intelligence.

Chapter 9 in this edition contains summaries of several chapters from the first edition. While these enablers are all useful, including them in the book made it significantly longer. Each is now summarized with a link and QR code to go to an online page where additional information can be found.

I would like to thank Mary Beth Ray, Pearson and IBM Press for their help resolving copyright issues so I could publish this updated version as well as Peter Fingar and the team at MK Press for publishing it.

My particular thanks go to the team at Decision Management Solutions who have worked with me on the projects that have field tested and refined the approach – Meri Gruber, Gagan Saxena, Ryan Trollip, Don Perkins, Charlotte DeKeyrel, Zoe Zhou, Dennis Siu, Mastan, Amulya, Lalitha, Srilatha, Ujjawal, Anil, Devi, and the rest of the development team. I would like to recognize Paul Buhler, Jan Purchase, Odd Steen, Stephen StPeter and Melanie Zimmerman for their detailed comments.

I would also like to acknowledge those who helped work on the first edition. Erick Brethenoux (now of Gartner) and Jean Pommier of IBM; Dr. Jeremy Bloom, Jerome Boyer, Dr Asit Dan, Sarah Dunworth, Michael McRoberts, Martha Mesa, Dr. Gregor Ottoson, Vijay Pandiarajan, Caroline Poser, David Pugh, Bruno Trimouille and Cheryl Wilson. I would also like to recognize Deepak Advani and Pierre Haren for their support getting the first edition published.

Any remaining errors or omissions are my own.

James Taylor

CEO, Decision Management Solutions

james@decisionmanagementsolutions.com

1. Artificial Intelligence

Artificial Intelligence is likely to change our civilization as much as or more than any technology that's come before, even writing
—Miles Brundage and Joanne Bryson, in Slate Magazine

The AI Opportunity

AI will add $13T to the global economy over the next decade
—Building the AI Powered Organization, HBR July-2019

97% of firms are investing in big data and artificial intelligence (AI)
—2018 survey by New Vantage Partners

Three-quarters of executives believe AI will enable their companies to move into new businesses. Almost 85% believe AI will allow their companies to obtain or sustain a competitive advantage.
—Reshaping Business With Artificial Intelligence, MIT Sloan Management Review September 06, 2017

76% [believed AI] will "substantially transform" their companies within the next 3 years
—Tom Davenport, The AI Advantage

There is an algorithm revolution underway as companies adopt predictive analytics, machine learning and other artificial intelligence (AI) technologies across their businesses. Increasingly it will be algorithms, not people, that make the decisions that matter to an organization. These algorithms use a variety of approaches to develop insight from data to ensure the organization makes decisions as profitably, effectively and efficiently as possible.

This revolution is being driven by better algorithms, more powerful computers, cloud computing and, most importantly, digital data. Information systems store information about almost every transaction. Websites generate digital "exhaust" about visitors, logging every page displayed or ad clicked on. Social media sites, reviews, and discussions create an unstructured his-tory of conversations about products, companies, people, and happenings. There has been an explosion of audio, image, and video data as digital cameras and equipment replace analog versions.

In theory, all this information is so useful to organizations that "data is the new oil". Companies increasingly see their data as a source of potential competitive advantage. New alliances and networks are forming to bring disparate data sources together and services are being offered for "free" in return for the right to collect and use the data being entered.

The promise is that algorithms can turn this data into insight that can help determine which among a company's products a consumer is most interested in, which transactions are fraudulent or wasteful, or which manufacturing tasks are likely to introduce quality problems. It can show what people really think about a product, predict what someone will do in a situation before they have even seen it and even drive cars.

The potential value of this data is great, but so is the scale of problem. The volume of data has become so large that only information systems can handle it. Not only must information systems be used to store and manage this information, they also must be used to analyze and act on it. Its scale simply exceeds the ability of people to cope. Digitizing our data leads us inevitably to digitizing the decisions we want to improve with that data.

Defining AI

Artificial intelligence – AI – is going to transform business. That is certainly its potential, at least when you apply it to deliver Digital Decisioning. But what, exactly, is AI? Is it just advanced machine learning? Is it only certain algorithms? Is it just a set of technology allowing a computer to interact in a human-like way?

Many frameworks exist for categorizing AI techniques. [1] Most consider two main classes of AI technologies – those related to

---

[1] Such as the one published by Gartner "Artificial Intelligence Hype: Managing Business Leadership Expectations", 5 June 2018 ID: G00343734, Erick Brethenoux or the one defined by Pedro Domingos, in The Master Algorithm 2015.

interfacing with humans and the world, and those related to decision-making as shown in Figure 1-1.

AI is often used to handle more natural forms of interfacing with computers. These replace forms, menus and buttons with more human-like interactions. They provide Natural Language Processing (NLP) to support conversational interfaces like chatbots. They recognize images of the real world, or of written words to identify signs, locations, damage and much else. They can transcribe audio (and then understand the resulting language) and support complex searches. All this "Interface AI" makes it easier for you to interact with your computer systems.

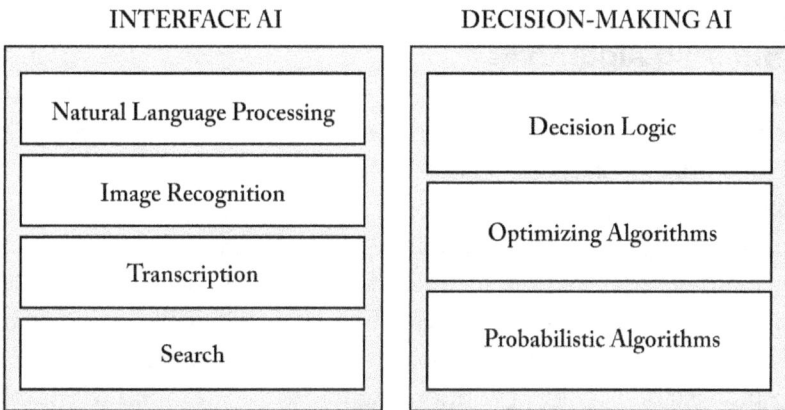

INTERFACE AI	DECISION-MAKING AI
Natural Language Processing	Decision Logic
Image Recognition	Optimizing Algorithms
Transcription	
Search	Probabilistic Algorithms

Figure 1-1: Types of AI

The second kind of AI makes decisions. This kind of AI often gets less attention but is central to creating business value. When people talk about using AI to improve marketing, handle claims, manage risk, detect fraud, reduce maintenance costs, streamline business processes and generally improve the stodgy old businesses it is "Decision-making AI" that is required. Three kinds of AI techniques make decisions.

Decision Logic

When AI was first discussed the approach used was to develop so-called "expert systems." These systems took what experts knew and codified it, so the system "knew" what the experts knew. These original expert systems evolved into systems based on well-managed business rules as well as systems for managing tabular logic or decision tables, decision trees, heuristic logic, and even fuzzy logic.

All these approaches involve representing the way a decision should be made explicitly. The decision logic might represent a policy that should be applied, a regulation that must be followed, or just best practices learned over time. The logic takes known data about a situation, a customer or a transaction and draws some conclusion about it. Business rules might decide if an application for a loan is complete or a decision tree might allocate a customer to one of several market segments.

For our purposes we are going to call all these technologies Business Rules as it is Business Rules Management Systems that dominate this sector of AI.

Optimizing Algorithms

Another AI thread grew up around using mathematics to find optimal solutions to problems. When a problem has multiple constraints and competing targets, people often make sub-optimal choices. Optimization or constraint-based approaches such as linear programming, solvers and genetic algorithms have been developed to use mathematical models to find either optimal solutions – the best possible set of results given the constraints - or plausible solutions that meet the constraints for situations in which any solution that works is acceptable. For instance, a solution might identify the minimum number of trucks required to deliver a set of packages in a specific time window given the delivery locations or it might suggest a possible work schedule given the need for specific nursing skills at specific times from a known pool of nurses.

These approaches require mathematical models to be developed that represent the relationships of inputs, decisions, outputs and measures of success. They need some data to support simulation and testing of the model but you don't need to analyze large volumes of data to develop them.

For our purposes we are going to call these technologies Optimization and the algorithms themselves Optimization Models.

Probabilistic Algorithms

The most recent and increasingly dominant thread in AI is that related to probabilistic or statistical decision-making techniques such as machine learning, predictive analytic modeling, deep learning, neural networks, and Bayesian nets. These techniques are a mixture of some very old techniques (Bayes for instance dates from the 1760s) and much newer ones. All these techniques work best when large amounts of data can be analyzed. The digital data and the compute power necessary to process all this data have only recently become available to most companies. This has driven the recent explosion of interest in these techniques

What they all have in common is that they determine a probability – how likely something is. An algorithm might predict how likely a machine is to fail in the next 24 hours or how likely a customer is to accept a particular offer. These predictions can be very powerful, but they are probabilities, not definitive statements.

It should be noted that some of the mathematical techniques used in interface AI, such as Natural Language Processing, can also be used to determine a probability. The same technique is used for both purposes but the difference in outcome makes it worth separating them.

For our purposes we are going to refer to these as Machine Learning techniques and the resulting algorithms as Predictive Analytic Models.

The AI Challenge

Gartner's 2018 CIO survey points to the fact that, although 86% of respondents indicate that they either have AI on their radar, or have initiated projects, only 4% have projects currently deployed.

In a 2017 McKinsey survey with 3,000+ respondents, only 20% had adopted one AI technology in one part of their business

There's a misconception that it's always going to be better to let an algorithm determine a solution, but that won't always be the case. AI isn't a good fit for every sort of problem.
—Building the AI Powered Organization, HBR July 2019
The gap between ambition and execution is large at most companies… only about one in five companies has incorporated AI in some offerings or processes. Only one in 20 companies has extensively incorporated AI in

offerings or processes. Across all organizations, only 14% of respondents believe that AI is currently having a large effect on their organization's offerings.

—Susan Athey, Economics of Technology Professor at Stanford Graduate School of Business, quoted in MIT Sloan Management Review September 06, 2017

There are relatively few examples of radical transformation with cognitive technologies actually succeeding, and many examples of "low hanging fruit" being successfully picked

—Tom Davenport AI Advantage

Many organizations' efforts with [AI] are falling short. Most firms have run only adhoc pilots or are applying AI in just a single business process… Firms struggle to move from the pilots to companywide programs

—Building the AI Powered Organization, HBR July 2019

Many managers and executives have become justifiably cynical about technology. Many assume that the potential of the latest technology is being oversold by well-funded start-ups and ivory-tower pundits. AI is just the latest example with many being told they must use artificial intelligence to "innovate" and become "data driven". They must change their business model, rip up established ways of doing things, "change or die."

This is not as easy as it might seem. AI is both tremendously powerful and massively over-hyped. The potential is real and great, but the reality is that most companies are failing miserably to apply AI. Most case studies are of pilots or experiments. They are full of words like "should" and "will" and "when fully deployed." Few companies can point to broad, deep deployments of AI.

The problem is that AI vendors and consultants are encouraging companies to put the technology first. They talk about "AI programs" and act as though adopting the technology is the same as delivering a business solution. They centralize control of these technologies away from those who understand the business, its drivers and its constraints. They talk as though people will be able to just do what the algorithms tell them to do.

This rarely works. Start-ups and "born digital" companies may be able to "pivot" and be "agile," changing the way they operate completely when the algorithms suggest they should. Large, established companies cannot. They must continue to sell insurance, offer banking products, make vehicles, manage money, produce drugs, deliver healthcare and ship products. They must just do this more effectively, more efficiently and with greater control. As Jeff Bezos said in his letter to Amazon shareholders in 2017:

"Much of the impact of machine learning will be of this type – quietly but meaningfully improving core operations"

What these big, traditional, somewhat boring companies need is a business-centric and realistic way to deliver value from AI. One that will let them quietly build more effective and efficient operations while retaining control. One that will put AI to work.

Digital decisioning is the most effective way to deliver the business value of AI. It may well be the **only** way for most large companies to deliver this value.

Enterprises waste time and money on unactionable analytics and rigid applications. Digital decisioning can stop this insanity. It is the highest-value next step for firms that wish to complete the insight-to-action cycle necessary for a successful digital transformation[2].

---

[2] The Dawn Of Digital Decisioning: New Software Automates Immediate Insight-To-Action Cycles Crucial For Digital Business by John R. Rymer and Mike Gualtieri, Forrester Research April 2018

2. Digital Decisioning

Digital decisioning lets you put your data to work targeting customers, managing risk, crushing fraud and focusing resources. It lets you adapt and change to continuously improve, test and learn, manage tradeoffs and move from machine learning to business learning. It puts you in control to enable rapid change, effective compliance and process improvement.

All the stories in this chapter are real. Names have been changed and some are composites of several companies, but all are inspired by real events.

Put Data To Work

Target customers

The head of marketing at a leading growth-focused insurance provider in Asia needed to increase the top-line value of each sale its agents make to their customers. Each agent interaction costs money and takes time to schedule, so profitable growth means taking maximum advantage of every interaction. While its best agents added additional products and optional extensions to the base products customers wanted, most agents did not. Her data showed that various combinations and product sequences are effective with different customer types but it wasn't clear to her how to use this analytic insight to drive improved results across a large agency force. It seemed a wasted opportunity.

The agents already used a mobile app to work directly with potential customers to enter information on the customer's financial needs, employment and payment capacity. Based on this information and a conversation with the customer, the agents recommend the best possible product for the customer. The value proposition is discussed, the costs outlined and the customer signs to send the application in for underwriting. This process relied on the agents to maximize the value of the sale while ensuring the customer got products they needed and could afford.

The head of marketing identified "next best offer" as the right approach to increase the value of these interactions. A next best offer program identifies the offer that will add the most value to a customer based on everything you know about them. She knew her analytics gave her great insight into her customers. Her data wasn't perfect, but it was good enough to give her the insights she needed to add value to each customer interaction. Getting thousands of agents to change their behavior would be hard, though. She'd also have to ensure that the offers were compliant with local regulations. And the offers must be delivered while the agents were talking to the customer. Getting through these roadblocks was going to take a new approach. A mentor pointed her to digital decisioning and provided some pilot funding.

The digital decisioning project was a complete success. It increased the top line value of these deals, the total annual premium. Tightly integrated with the mobile app, the solution used the customer data entered during the current interaction, applied advanced segmentation and propensity-to-purchase analytics to categorize the customer, and applied suitability and product rules to determine the right next product for the customer.

Thanks to digital decisioning, she knows customers will see the best offer available for the right product. A compelling description of the offer is presented to the customer directly in the app. Nearly a quarter of the customers accept the offer and this number has risen steadily since the system went live. When they do, they can immediately add it to their basket.

Digital decisioning means she is certain that its always an attractive offer. It's never a product the customer already has or have already asked for. It's never incompatible with the products they are considering. It always considers which products are available to people like them. It doesn't pick things they're not likely to be underwritten for. It picks the best out of what's possible, every time, in real-time. It doesn't just use the company's data; it uses its institutional knowledge and regulatory context to make sure the product is the right one.

The results have been impressive. After an initial pilot, this was adopted by a remarkable 98% of the agents. The agents appreciated both the precision of the targeting and the seamless way it was integrated. Plus, it never embarrassed them by offering something irrelevant. By slightly increasing the size of so many deals, she's generated millions of dollars in additional premium in the first year, over and above the cost of the system. The incremental value of this new business is very high as the costs are almost zero. As the CFO observed, the ROI is enormous and the effort tiny.

Next best offer delivers a more targeted and customized customer experience. Making sure every interaction makes the right offer to each customer at the right time is hard. Digital decisioning makes it easy.

This story illustrates one of the key characteristics of digital decisioning. Digital decisioning is analytic, using the data you have or can acquire to drive more effective and profitable decisions for your organization. Digital decisioning is not about reporting on this data or even about analyzing this data. It is about using this data to act analytically on behalf of your users.

Our head of marketing used digital decisioning to target customers. Others have used digital decisioning to manage risk, crush fraud and maximize the value of scarce resources.

Manage Risk

Managing risks like credit risk, delivery risk and underwriting risk is one of the leading use cases for digital decisioning. For instance, one leading property and casualty insurance company with over $20B in net premiums implemented digital decisioning to manage risk in business insurance, specifically products for small businesses (those with fewer than 50 employees).

The small business insurance market is competitive, and they identified that getting products to market quickly, offering more sophisticated and granular pricing, responding to changes quickly, and being easier to do business with would all help them grow.

The previous policy processing system couldn't support automated underwriting and pricing. Only 17% of their small commercial policies qualified for straight thru processing, and rules could not be changed quickly. Crucially, the old system was also unable to differentiate between risks, so it priced them all the same. This led the company to become a victim of "adverse selection."

> **Adverse Selection**
>
> When an insurer prices in a less granular way than its competitors, it acquires an unusually high number of "bad" customers. The process works like this: Within a pricing tier, all customers get the same price. Some of these customers are less risky than the average for the group and some are more risky. If another company offers several price tiers to this same group of customers, the more risky customers will tend not to switch as their price will be better if they stay. Lower risk customers will likely get a better price from the competitor and will leave. The effect is that a company "selects" more bad risks when its risk pricing is less granular than its competitors.

As part of a comprehensive quote-to-issue platform they use digital decisioning for underwriting. A predictive analytic model to target pricing based on risk was built from three years' worth of data. This new risk model was wrapped with business rules to ensure that the right policies and regulations were applied and that models could drive completely automated underwriting decisions. Every quote is now saved for future analysis so the models can be refined based on results.

For this organization, digital decisioning increased the written premium by 50%. Straight through processing rose to 75% resulting in an increase in overall business flow of 73%. The number of agents quoting increased by nearly 20% the number of quotes per agent increased 25% and the submission flow increased 50%.

Crush Fraud

One critical area for fraud and compliance in banking is detecting and preventing money laundering. After the passage of stricter money laundering reporting requirements and an acquisition that substantially enlarged it, a major bank needed to develop a new approach. Under its old decentralized system, staff routinely had to analyze over 100,000 customers and transactions per year. Despite this huge amount of analysis, only a few hundred reports of suspicious operation were filed with the government, and only just over half of them achieved the government's highest quality and thoroughness rating.

The bank applied machine learning to its transactional data to identify suspicious transactions that may have resulted from money laundering or terrorism financing. The resulting predictive analytic model powered digital decisioning that flagged customers and transactions as suspicious, applying government regulations and other best practices as well as machine learning. This analytical digital decisioning produced rapid, significant benefits for the bank. It enabled its specialized analysis unit to narrow its focus to smaller, more precise segments. From over 100,000 analyses they were able to focus on just a few thousand identified by the system. Despite this twenty-fold reduction the bank increased the number of suspicious operation reports filed with the government threefold and immensely improved the quality; so now nearly all meet the highest rating in terms of quality and thoroughness.

An unsought but welcome benefit has been huge productivity savings generated by this new approach. The bank has been able to redeploy nearly 1,000 team members with 80 percent of those resources now focused on bringing new business into the bank and improving the bottom line. Being able to focus staff on the business as a whole rather than on transaction handling is a typical benefit of digital decisioning.

Fraud is also an issue in insurance, where detecting and handling fraudulent claims is critical to overall profitability. A provider of nonstandard personal automobile insurance that emphasizes higher-risk drivers, depends on its ability to identify fraudulent claims for sustained profitability. Following the implementation of digital decisioning, they have doubled the accuracy of fraud identification, contributing to a return on investment of over 400%. In addition to increasing the accuracy of fraud identification, the referral time to send those claims to the Special Investigative Unit has gone from 45–60 days down to 1–3 days, and customer service has been enhanced through fast payment of legitimate claims, contributing to above-average company growth.

This digital decisioning approach combines predictive analytics with business rules and what-if analysis in a single system. The system allows business users to ensure the best possible outcome by defining and performing "what if" simulations and adjusting the parameters for different situations. Business managers can also quickly modify business rules and see their changes deployed immediately, giving them the flexibility to make adjustments as business needs change. As a result, claims adjustors and others with in-depth business knowledge can quickly and easily define how risk should be assessed and automate many routine decisions while retaining full control of the claims handling process.

Focus Resources

Digital decisioning can automatically focus constrained resources on the right problem, maximizing the value an organization gets from those resources. One airport management organization must allocate physical resources from gates and airplane parking stands to luggage conveyer belts and check-in counters for over 1,000 flights across several airports. It needs to prevent congestion in the air and on the ground so that more than 150,000 air travelers can flow smoothly through the airports. Manual decision-making for a problem of this complexity results in under-utilized and poorly allocated resources. It also takes too long. The manual process for allocating flights to gates, for instance, used to take several hours.

Digital decisioning allows them to handle this complexity. The system allocates parking stands to flights while considering everything from security and fuel handling to airline preferences and schedules. Once the best solution is found, all the primary ground resources like buses and gates are also assigned. The system considers long term trends too, assuring continuity for airlines so they can become familiar with their assignments.

The system does all this in just minutes. This means the staff has more time to check and fine-tune the results and, more importantly, that it can be used to re-plan in the face of the unexpected. Now when equipment breaks down or the weather causes problems, the allocation of resources can be reassessed immediately to ensure the best possible response. Thanks to the system and its more effective allocation of resources, there are fewer flight delays, faster time through the airport for passengers and lower operating costs.

Adapt And Improve Results

Improve Continuously

The Chief Operating Officer at a leading health insurance provider has a well-deserved reputation for being cynical about technology. She's heard many grand promises from many software companies over the years. Too many of these promises have not been met, leaving her team to work nights and weekends picking up the pieces. At this point she's disbelieving almost everything said about new technology.

One day she was invited to a meeting by the Chief Customer Officer of the group. His focus was on improving customer satisfaction. He knew that one powerful way to do this was to handle medical claims more effectively. Customers whose claim is paid quickly and accurately are happier and likely to promote their insurance company. Those who wait and have to argue, much less so.

He knew that the company was investing in a mobile claims handling app, direct data connections to medical providers to support electronic submission of claims and AI-based chatbots so consumers could ask questions about their claims. He worried that if the claims being processed by these new systems still required manual review, much of the customer satisfaction benefit would be lost: The mobile app would only be able to say that a claim had been successfully submitted, automated submissions would still wait weeks for review and the chatbot would have nothing to say about a customer's specific claim. Without a minimum level of automation and straight through processing, customer satisfaction would stay low despite these new systems.

He invited the COO and her team to see how a digital decisioning system worked. Businesspeople working with the system showed how they could change its behavior, simulate the impact of a change and put it into production if they were happy with the result. They talked about the decisions the system made and how it reflected their view of the business. They showed how it used powerful descriptive and predictive analytics to make better decisions. And they showed how they could review decisions made by the system to make future improvements.

Despite her cynicism, the COO was impressed. Her systems for storing and processing claims had been digitized in recent years, but all the decision-making remained manual. With 100% of claims getting manual review, customer satisfaction with the claims process was low. In addition, costs were high, and it was hard to see how the process could scale to handle a growing number of consumers with medical insurance. All that said, she had been reluctant to throw technology at the problem. Her experience had made her cautious about technological solutions. But she saw that digital decisioning was a new approach. Its focus on business control, continuous improvement and the practical application of analytics resonated with her. This, she thought, could work.

The CCO's and COO's teams worked together to adopt digital decisioning to automate claims handling. Using a mixture of explicit business rules, business rules derived from data analysis and predictive risk analytics, a minimum viable product was developed and deployed. This focused on automatically paying the claims that everyone agreed should be paid. These obviously valid claims would be routed immediately for payment, regardless of the channel used to submit them (paper, electronic, web, mobile or chatbot).

The initial rate was much lower than the COO had set as her target. The head of claims knew the COO's target. She also knew that the company, like most insurance companies, is risk averse. Starting with only the most obvious claims helped manage the risk by limiting exposure. The use of digital decisioning ensured that the initial rate of straight through processing was just the beginning. She had seen how the approach provides a comprehensive platform for continuous improvement.

Each week the head of claims and her business team reviewed the claims that had been sent for manual adjudication that week. She and her team could see exactly how the claims handling decision has been made for each claim. They identify changes in the decision-making that will increase the rate of straight through processing. Without any IT support, the team can simulate the impact of these changes using a year's worth of historical data. She knows this impact analysis will reassure everyone that the increase in the system's scope will not create problems. This impact report can be reviewed with the COO and other stakeholders. With their approval, her team can push weekly changes into production. The claims process stays the same and the multiple customer facing channels all stay the same – just the decision changes.

After 10 weeks of continuous improvement the head of claims could tell the COO that they had comfortably exceeded their original target. Since then, the claims team has established a regular cadence of using data to improve their business decisions. In less than a year their straight through processing rate is more than double their original target and is still growing. The head of claims is happy as costs fall and accuracy is up. The chief customer officer is happy too because customer satisfaction is up, with more customers than ever getting their money quickly and with less paperwork. And the COO has finally found a technology that didn't disappoint.

Being customer centric is not just about delivering marketing offers and improving sales interactions. Customer satisfaction is often driven by more practical interactions, like claims handling. If your customers feel like their claims are being handled poorly or taking too long, they are unlikely to think positively about you even if you make great marketing offers. Handling claims and other moments of truth well is essential to ensure your customers feel you are putting them front and center. Keeping existing customers is just as important as finding new ones.

This story illustrates the second key characteristic of digital decisioning. Digital decisioning is adaptive, helping you learn what works and continuously improve your approach.

In this case, our COO used digital decisioning to empower her team to drive continuous improvement. Others use digital decisioning for experimentation, to make progressively better tradeoffs, and to turn machine learning into business learning.

Test and Learn

One of the most important ways in which digital decisioning can be adaptive is in its support of test and learn experimentation. Digital decisioning allows multiple approaches to decision-making to be defined. These approaches are tested against each other in the only laboratory that works when you are trying to see how consumers will react—the real world.

One information solutions provider developed digital decisioning for credit risk decisioning that is licensed to financial services and other companies to help them manage credit accounts more profitably. One of the most powerful elements of this platform is how it supports a test and learn approach.

Within the system a bank or credit union can define multiple credit policies. These policies define what credit limit might be approved for an account, when a credit line increase might be appropriate or what kind of credit product should be offered. The financial institution sets up a default approach and identifies the others for testing. What-if analysis tools compare the approaches and estimate the likely difference between them based on past results.

Just because what-if analysis identifies an approach as superior, does not mean it will actually work better when it is tried on real customers. As many companies have found out to their detriment, consumers are not entirely predictable. Instead of relying on offline analysis, the system allows institutions to test new approaches in the real world. As consumers apply for credit from the financial institution most are processed using the default approach while some are processed using one of the test approaches. The system carefully tracks which approach was used for which consumer. As time passes the institution gathers information about which approach works best—which results in the lowest rate of default, highest rate of usage and greatest customer satisfaction for instance.

Once the results are in for the test groups the institution can run reports and do analysis to see how the overall results would look if the different approaches were applied to everyone. From this the institution learns which approach it should use in the future. The agility of digital decisioning means it is easy to change the default approach to the one with the best results and also easy to create new approaches to see if they will be even better. A never-ending cycle of continuous improvement can begin.

Manage Trade-offs

Digital decisioning can help organizations find new approaches and conduct experiments to test and learn what works or will work best. As decisions become more complex, as there are more objectives to be considered and more data about what might work, it becomes essential that they also manage complex tradeoffs.

One company uses digital decisioning to help airlines manage their operations and provides other services for travel companies. Airline planning and operations decisions are driven by the desire to minimize operating cost while simultaneously maximizing operating profit. Airlines have access to limited resources (aircraft, crew, airport systems) so effective planning is essential for profitability and survival.

For instance, daily airline schedules are rarely flown as planned due to weather, air traffic control, labor unrest, mechanical problems and security procedures. Disruptions can have a significant impact on operations due to the complex interactions between aircraft, flight crews and passengers. When schedules are disrupted, there is often no "good" answer, only complex tradeoffs to make. Digital decisioning help airlines better manage off-schedule operations and disruptions while providing them with the ability to re-accommodate passengers and thus improve the overall passenger travel experience.

Schedules are not the only place where airlines must manage complex tradeoffs. With customers increasingly price driven and booking closer to departure, airline travel has become a more dynamic marketplace. This conflicts with traditional revenue management systems which assume more stable patterns of customer purchasing behavior. This company also delivers digital decisioning to help manage the revenue management tradeoffs in this new environment. These systems determine the set of revenue management controls that will maximize revenue given the current competitive situation and airline data. Strategic objectives can be fed into the digital decisioning environment to determine feasible revenue management actions given all the various tradeoffs.

This more complex revenue management environment extends to travel agencies. Faced with declining commissions and increasing competition, agencies must strike and manage incentive deals that pay override commissions or guarantee fare discounts. Digital decisioning also evaluates pending supplier deals and constructs the best possible supplier deal portfolio from them. This allows agencies to manage and drive demand to maximize revenue. The same system also provides appropriate sales targets given the current set of supplier deals. This system allows agencies to negotiate better supplier deals and reduces deal conflicts while providing the right sales targets.

From Machine Learning to Business Learning

Machine learning is a key component of artificial intelligence. The ability of machine learning algorithms to process new data and adjust the factors that drive their outcomes is one of their defining characteristics. This can be used periodically to update an analytic model, in credit risk for example. It can also be used continuously, as it might be in spam filters or other fraud detection scenarios.

These algorithms are typically just one element in a business decision, however. Take predictive maintenance. Applying machine learning to sensor data from machines creates an algorithm that predicts how likely a particular machine is to fail in a specific time period. Sensor data flows in continually and is used to keep learning – the algorithm is refined as data is received.

How can this prediction be used to drive better business outcomes? One company wanted to reduce its maintenance costs and improve its uptime. These predictions were a key part of its approach. It used them to drive a critical decision – whether a machine needed to be maintained today or not.

The prediction was not the only element though. Some machines required very specialized staff for maintenance who were not available every day. Some machines had requirements for regular scheduled maintenance driven by contracts and warranty agreements. If an engineer was going to be at one machine, it would be easy to look at nearby machines too so lower thresholds could be set. There was, as always, a whole decision to wrap about the prediction.

Digital decisioning combined the various elements of this decision into a single component. Using this to drive maintenance tasks made the engineering team much more efficient. Analyzing the data produced let them learn about their business. How often did they predict that they should maintain a machine but found there was no engineer available? What was the value of the extra uptime from the machines who's predicted maintenance needs could be met and those where predicted maintenance was delayed? Was that value enough to pay for additional specialists? Machine learning driving business learning.

Be In Control

Rapid Change

The head of originations at a major retail lender was struggling with the originations system they had. This system took all the applications for credit from consumers and handled all the steps up through making funds or credit available. The system processed all these applications just fine. The problem was how it decided which ones to approve and which products to offer.

Decisions about credit origination are often complex. They're typically more than just yes/no decisions, with credit limits and product conditions having to be selected for each application. They involve many eligibility criteria, detailed segmentation, complex risk scoring, affordability calculations and much more. He was finding it more and more difficult to keep the system up to date and aligned with the bank's risk strategy and product portfolio. The origination system was just too closed and inflexible. This meant that too many applications required manual review. For some online and mobile products this was completely unacceptable and even for more traditional products, consumers increasingly expect a real-time response. They want their store card to be approved while they shop, for instance.

Realizing that only the decision itself needed to change, he initiated an effort to separate out everything that had to do with making decisions from the previously monolithic application. Because how the bank decides was the highest change piece of the system, being able to change it more frequently had tremendous business value. Applying digital decisioning meant that the decision became a separate "product" with its own lifecycle.

He also wanted his business users empowered to make changes to the decision. The new system exposed the core decision logic in ways that were accessible to those with the domain expertise so they could make changes themselves. Editing controls, validation, verification and testing made sure that the new logic would work. Powerful impact analysis tools meant that the impact of any change on the customer portfolio and overall risk and default levels would be clear before they were deployed. That way the business owners could be sure their changes would work as intended.

With the new system in place his business team was able to make and test logic changes in just a couple of days, down from over one to two months! And that's just because of the thoroughness of the testing and impact analysis. The change itself takes just minutes. Because the system is more current, more aligned with the business, manual referrals for review dropped by 75%.

But the most interesting thing he found was how this kind of system changes the way business people think. It turns out that if it takes months to get a change implemented, most businesspeople being conservative, they tend to automate less and refer more to manual review. They experiment less and try fewer of those good ideas that bubble up from time to time. The effort to make a change deters them from actually making a change.

Newly empowered to drive rapid change his business partners make changes more often than before. Even when something is a little "out there" as an approach, they are confident they can evaluate the business impact in advance and quickly make adjustments. Even if it doesn't work quite the way they thought it would, when it is released into the wild. When someone suggests using a new data source to identify risky customers, it can be rapidly evaluated. If it works, it can be rolled out across products quickly because digital decisioning is a central, shared service.

The impact of this empowerment? Millions of dollars in savings per year, better customer service and more innovative credit products. Rapid change, agility, is not just about responding to new regulations or competitive product launches. When the business feels in control, innovation is unleashed.

This story illustrates the final key characteristic of digital decisioning. Digital decisioning is agile, ensuring that the business can make the changes it needs to make when it needs to make them.

This case should how our head of originations used digital decisioning to support rapid and effective change. Others use digital decisioning to ensure compliance and innovate business processes.

Effective Compliance

Digital decisioning offers safe agility—an ability to make the right changes quickly. Particularly, when systems must be compliant with external regulations or internal policies. A leading provider of prescription benefit programs works with an expansive network of pharmacies nationwide. It provides prescription drug programs and specialized services to organizations across the public and private sectors.

One of the critical services they provide to their customers (health care insurance plans) is the processing and settling of prescription drug claims. How well a claim transaction is handled can impact everything from service commitments and regulatory compliance to a plan's profitability and ability to attract and retain members. As a pharmacy benefits management company, they need a claims system that supports a complex distribution channel, delivers customized programs, and meets changing market and regulatory demands.

By implementing digital decisioning, the company improved collaboration between business and IT by allowing senior pharmacist business users to work with a business analyst to define, test, create, and maintain the many rules that determine which claims should be paid. These rules validate member, claim and clinical data as well as handling segmentation and assignment; adjudication, payment and settlement. These rules are compliant with regulations that vary from state to state, as well Federal regulations such as the Health Insurance Portability and Accountability Act (HIPAA).

The new claims system delivered time-to-market gains of over 70 percent, a reduction in claims processing time and costs by 30 percent and an increase in straight through processing of over 80 percent. They can roll out new programs and add members faster and demonstrate its compliance, thanks to comprehensive audit trails of business rules and decisions rendered at any given time.

Process Improvement

The head of the call center at an international provider of voice and data telecommunications in Asia understood the importance of delighting customers. He wanted to take every opportunity to personalize his customers' experience even before they interacted with his staff. He was already applying digital decisioning to route calls that came into the call center. Using information about the caller, the services they already had and the kind of problem they said they were experiencing, digital decisioning routed calls to an appropriate service agent. Customers really liked being sent directly to an agent who could help them.

But he wanted to do more. He knew how important it was for the company to sell value added services to customers. This was a priority for the company, so every call to the call center ended with an attempt to make a cross-sell or up-sell. He immediately saw this as another opportunity to use digital decisioning.

Like all good next best offer approaches, his team used predictive analytics and machine learning to build models to predict which value-added service would be the most compelling upsell for each customer. Combined with eligibility and suitability rules, these predictions maximized acceptance rates by ensuring the call center representatives knew which offer to make at the end of each support call. Every offer was targeted and personalized to the particular customer.

While this delivered great results, he realized he could go further. Some call center staff were much better at selling certain services. Perhaps they had some connection to the service, valued it themselves or knew someone who really liked it. Because he had digitized the decision about which offer to make, the head of the call center realized it could be embedded earlier in the customer journey.

Now calls are routed to a representative who can help with the technical problem and who is *also* good at selling the offer identified for that customer. The technical problem comes first, so that it gets handled quickly and effectively. Where possible the call gets handled by someone who is also more likely to succeed in the upsell. This boosts the success rate even further. It also improves morale in the call center because representatives are generally being asked to sell services they believe in.

Moving decisions earlier in the process or earlier in the customer journey like this makes them more targeted. It makes them more streamlined and can even radically reshape them. Digital decisioning is a powerful tool for digital transformation, even in people-centric processes like the call center.

Digital Decisioning Defined

Digital decisioning software capitalizes on analytical insights and machine learning models about customers and business operations to automate actions (including advising a human agent) for individual customers through the right channels.[3]

Businesses must make choices, business decisions, on a regular basis. Each selection or calculation of an outcome depends on a set of data inputs. The decisions an organization makes ultimately have an observable impact on the behavior of the organization and on its results.

A digital decision is a decision made "in silico" – made automatically by a computer.

The stories above illustrate the key characteristics of digital decisioning. Digital decisioning embeds analytic insight to make more precise, more profitable decisions. Digital decisioning is adaptive, responding to new data and continuously improving your results. Digital decisioning is agile, putting the business in control and delivering safe, compliant agility.

Digital decisions are repeatable, operational, "micro" decisions that lead automatically to actions. They decide how to interact with customers and how to handle transactions. They allow an organization to determine the right way to handle high volume transactions or interactions when making this determination is not easy or obvious and when responsiveness and scale are critical.

Digital Decisioning is a key element of a digital business, transforming the customer experience, managing risk, crushing fraud and reshaping operations. Applied effectively, digital decisioning adds personalization and customization while delivering self-service and support for mobile, chat bots and new voice interfaces. It works 24x7 and can be scaled up as necessary, providing extraordinary levels of cost effectiveness as companies grow and expand. Most importantly, it lets

---

[3] The Dawn Of Digital Decisioning New Software Automates Immediate Insight-To-Action Cycles Crucial For Digital Business by John R. Rymer and Mike Gualtieri April 2018 Forrester

organizations finally get a return from their investment in analytic algorithms, machine learning and AI.

Digital decisioning works for a wide range of use cases if you use the right approach, one focused specifically on delivering the value of digital decisioning: Decision Management delivers digital decisioning. Described in the following chapters, Decision Management is a proven framework for effectively applying AI technologies such as business rules, machine learning and optimization.

Digital Decisioning improves accuracy in decision-making by applying machine learning and optimization to make more data-driven decisions. More fine-grained and customized decisions, focusing on individual customers or transactions, allow for more accurate and specific risk management and more targeted customer treatment.

Digital Decisioning uses business rules to ensure that policies are applied consistently across different channels, different business processes and over time. This results in fewer fines, lower audit and legal costs and improved customer satisfaction.

Digital Decisioning's use of business rules also allows for more rapid response to business threats and means fewer missed opportunities. It also helps organizations cope with imposed changes such as new regulations. The time and cost to make changes is reduced. The traceability of change and the ability to simulate its likely impact make it more likely that an organization will "risk" a change because they are more confident in its outcome.

Digital Decisioning allows greater throughput and increases customer satisfaction. Taking an action sooner often adds value too by making a response more likely or reducing carrying costs.

Digital Decisioning drives down costs by eliminating the need for manual decision-making. This cost benefit is multiplied by the volume of the decision.

Digital Decisioning adds additional value thanks to its focus on continuous improvement. Organizations can improve the quality of their decision-making over time. They can identify and change poorly performing, redundant, inconsistent and out of date decisions quickly and easily.

Organizations that have adopted Digital Decisioning have gained tremendous results from doing so. Digital Decisioning has kept companies profitable despite the risks they face and has maximized the value of their customers. It has allowed organizations to learn from their successes and failures, and continuously improve their business. It has also allowed them to avoid business risks and take advantage of narrow windows of opportunity. Any organization would want these benefits.

3. Digital Decisioning Principles

There are specific AI technologies involved in Digital Decisioning, but the use of these technologies is not sufficient. Four principles are at the heart of Digital Decisioning and must be applied to deliver the maximum return on a digital decisioning investment.

1 Begin with the decision in mind
Digital Decisioning has a central and ongoing focus on automating decisions, particularly operational and "micro" decisions.

2 Be transparent and agile
With Digital Decisioning, the way each decision is made is both explicable to non-technical professionals and easy to change.

3 Be predictive not reactive
Digital Decisioning uses data to improve the way decisions are being made by predicting probabilities and likely outcomes.

4 Test, learn and continually improve
Digital Decisioning assumes change and the way a decision is made is continually re-assessed to learn what works and adapted to work better.

Principle #1: Begin With The Decision in Mind

Most information systems are developed with a focus on business functions such as accounting, business data such as customer information, or business processes such as order to cash. These approaches share a common challenge: they assume either that *people* will make all the decisions involved in the functions and business processes being automated or that how these decisions are made can be fixed.

Digital Decisioning takes a different approach. It begins with the decision in mind and focuses on the automation and improvement of specific business decisions. As a decision involves selecting from a range of alternatives, Digital Decisioning automates that selection. The system chooses the action or actions that should be taken given the data available and the context of the decision. Digital Decisioning does not assume that every decision must always be taken by a human. It uses AI technologies like business rules, machine learning and optimization to make these decisions using the same business logic and analysis humans would apply but without human intervention.

Organizations can't and won't automate every decision. Only certain decisions are addressed by Digital Decisioning.

Repeatable Decisions

Information systems are good at handling repetitive tasks. They excel at doing the same thing over and over without variation and without making mistakes from one transaction to the next. Something that cannot be defined in a repeatable way is not a good target for any kind of information system. Only those decisions that are repeatable are good candidates for Digital Decisioning.

A repeatable decision is one that is made more than once by an organization following a well-defined, or at least definable, decision making approach. Business decisions can be categorized in various ways; one effective way to look at decisions is to categorize them as strategic, tactical, or operational (Taylor & Raden, 2007). This divides decisions into three categories based on the value of each decision made—the difference between a good and a bad decision—and the number of times such a decision is made by an organization:

- **Strategic decisions** are those high value, low volume decisions that guide the overall direction of the company. These ad-hoc, typically one-off decisions are made by senior management or the executive team of an organization. Lots of information is assembled and analyzed while many options are considered. Once the decision is made, it is never made again in the same context—later revision is really a different decision as circumstances are different. Organizations may know that a strategic decision is going to be needed well in advance, but often these decisions arise from unexpected opportunities or challenges. Strategic decisions are not candidates for Digital Decisioning as they lack the key element of repeatability.

- **Tactical decisions** are those focused on management and control. These medium value decisions still have significant business impact. They too involve data and analysis, typically by humans in management or knowledge worker positions.

46

These decisions do repeat—the same kind of decision is made repeatedly during normal business operations. Decisions about the discounting approach being used or the staffing levels of a call center are examples, and these decisions must be made every month or every week. The same or very similar analysis is performed each time, and company policies may play a significant role in how the decision is made. More repeatable and consistent tactical decisions are targets for Digital Decisioning.

- **Operational decisions** are those of lower individual value and typically relate to a single customer or a single transaction. They are critical to the effective operation of an organization, especially an organization of any size. Because of the number of times they must be made, consistency and repeatability are critical. Policies and well-defined decision-making criteria are typically developed to ensure this consistency. Despite their low individual value, they are extremely valuable in aggregate. A decision made thousands or millions or even billions of times a year has a total value that often exceeds even the most important strategic decision. Furthermore, strategic and tactical decisions (for example, to focus on customer retention or discount more aggressively) will only have an impact if a whole series of operational decisions (how to retain this customer or what discount to offer this distributor) are made in accordance with the higher level decision. For these reasons, operational decisions are the most common subject of Digital Decisioning.

To begin with the decision in mind, we must understand which decisions are to be the focus of any Digital Decisioning initiative.

Operational Decisions

Operational decisions are by far the most common kind of repeatable decision. Every order placed, every customer interaction, every claim or credit card transaction involves operational decisions. Operational decisions are the day-to-day, run-the-business decisions that are taken in large numbers by every organization.

Operational decisions are highly repeatable—in fact, being consistent by following a set of guidelines or applying the relevant policies and regulations is a defining characteristic of an operational decision. They can also involve an assessment of risk, as many forms of risk (loan default or credit risk, for instance) are acquired one transaction at a time. They must often be made in real-time or near real-time, while customers are waiting for the decision to be made.

While many operational decisions are made about customers, they can also be made about shipments, suppliers, or staff. As more physical devices are connected to the Internet with sensors or RFID chips, operational decisions are often made about "things"—about vehicles, packages, railcars or network components.

Business strategy and strategic decisions

This focus on repeatable, operational decisions can and should be combined with a focus on business strategy. A business strategy must be supported by many operational decisions if it is to be put into practice. For instance, if a focus on growing per-customer revenue is central to your business strategy then you have made a strategic decision to adopt this approach. There will be many operational decisions that will be influenced by and contribute to this strategy. For example, unless operational decisions about customer retention and cross-sell offers are made effectively you cannot deliver on this customer-centric strategy. As discussed in Chapter 5 the right operational decisions to focus on are those that support the objectives and key metrics of the organization.

Micro Decisions

Micro decisions are a particular kind of operational decision (Taylor & Raden, 2007) where the desire to personalize an interaction with a customer requires a focus on making a decision for that customer and that customer only. Often an operational decision is repeated for all customers, with the decision being based only on the data available for the particular interaction or transaction concerned. A micro decision, in contrast, uses everything known or predictable about a customer to make a unique decision just for them. Two customers making the same request or involved in identical transactions would get two different outcomes.

This focus on the information about the customer is what makes micro decisions a distinct form of operational decision. Everything known about the customer must be synthesized into actionable insight about the customer and fed into the operational decision alongside the information about the transaction. For example, when an order is placed, two operational decisions might be made—what shipping options to offer on the order and what discount to offer. The first of these might be managed as a standard operational decision with information about the order such as delivery address, weight, and value used to determine which of the various shipping options would be allowed. The second could be managed similarly but could also be handled as a micro decision. The customer's history with the company could be used to compute their likely future profitability and the risk that they might consider a competitor. This information, as well as information about the specific order, would then feed a micro decision to calculate a discount specific to *this* customer placing *this* order at *this* moment.

Principle #2: Be Transparent And Agile

Most information systems are opaque and hard to change. The use of code to specify their behavior makes them opaque to any but the most technically adept. It is also difficult to confirm that changes made to the code do what they are expected to do. Together, these characteristics make for long change cycles and a lack of responsiveness. Extensive Information Technology projects must be planned, budgeted, and executed to make changes to the behavior of a system.

These characteristics are unacceptable in Digital Decisioning. Opacity is unacceptable because many decisions must demonstrate that they are compliant with policies or regulations. If the code is opaque, then it will not be possible to see how decisions have been made and it will not be possible to verify that these decisions were correct or compliant. Digital Decisioning also involves decisions that are based on detailed business know-how and experience. If the code is so opaque that it cannot be understood by those who have this know-how or experience, then it is unlikely to be correct.

Organizational decision-making changes constantly so agility is also essential. As regulations change the behavior of any system that implements that regulation must change also. Organizations also want their Digital Decisioning investment to result in good decisions— effective ones. Effective decisions must meet the expectations of customers and be competitive in the aggregate. The behavior of competitors and customer expectations change constantly. Customers and competitors are not obliged to tell organizations when their expectations or plans change. An ability to rapidly change Digital Decisioning to respond is essential.

Digital Decisioning must therefore be both transparent and agile:

- The Digital Decisioning design must be transparent so that it is clear that the system is executing the behavior expected of it.

- The execution of Digital Decisioning must be transparent to allow reporting and continuous analysis of how decisions were made and the impact of this.

- Digital Decisioning systems must be agile so that their behavior can be changed when necessary without delay and without unnecessary expense.

Design Transparency and Why It Matters

Digital Decisioning requires design transparency. It must be possible for non-technical experts—those who understand the regulations or policies involved or who have the necessary know-how and experience—to determine if the system is going to behave as required. Those without IT expertise must be able to manage the way in which decisions are made so that it is clear to all participants involved. The drivers or source of this behavior must be identifiable so that those reviewing the behavior of the system can clearly assess its effectiveness in meeting objectives.

Tracking the source of decision-making behavior also means that changes in those sources can be quickly mapped to the changes required in the system. Design transparency means it is possible to determine the way in which a proposed change will ripple through. One regulatory change might impact many decisions for example and decisions may be dependent on the same data elements because they have information needs in common

Organizations must be sure that their systems will make decisions accurately and effectively after a change is made. This requires that the ripples and impacts of any change can be determined before it is made. Design transparency is essential to being able to trace these impacts.

Execution Transparency and Why It Matters

When a decision is made by a person, they can be asked to explain the decision. If a person rejects an application for a loan, for instance, they can be asked to appear in court, to write a letter explaining, or simply to answer the customer's questions. This is not possible when a system makes a decision. Digital Decisioning must ensure that explanations of decisions can be provided that will satisfy customers or suppliers who are materially affected by them. When a decision is regulated, such as when deciding which consumers may have access to credit, it must be possible to provide an exact description of how each decision was made so that it can be reviewed for compliance. Digital Decisioning requires real execution transparency in these cases.

Recent regulations have increased the need for execution transparency to the point where even marketing and promotional decisions must be explicable. Some decisions may not require execution transparency even today. When deciding when to bring a human into the loop, for fraud investigation for instance, it may not be necessary to understand why as the human acts as a second "pair of eyes."

As machine learning and other more opaque AI techniques are used in Digital Decisioning, the need for execution transparency increases. It is important that any predictive analytic model included in the system can explain its execution. This explanation must be wrapped with an explanation of how the whole decision was made and how that decision depended on the predictive analytic model.

Even if execution transparency is not required, an understanding of how each decision was made is a driver for continuous improvement and will help improve the decision-making of the system. Knowledge of how decisions were made can be aggregated to identify opportunities for improvement. Any approach to Digital Decisioning must support execution transparency as well as design transparency.

Business Agility and Why It Matters

An increase in transparency is likely to result in an increase in business agility. If it is easier to see how something works, it will be easier to change how it works. A faster response to a needed change improves overall business agility. Transparency is necessary for agility but not sufficient. Once a change is identified and its design impact assessed, it must be possible to make the change quickly and reliably. Digital Decisioning can require real-time changes in extreme cases. Daily or weekly changes are very common. When sudden market changes occur, such as major bankruptcies or an outbreak of hostilities, the resulting need for changes can be extreme. Money—and perhaps lives—will be lost every minute until the change is made.

Agile decision-making for truly agile processes

Many organizations invest a great deal in developing agile business processes. Digital Decisioning further increases this agility as business changes often involve updates to business decisions. These decisions are often the most dynamic part of a process, the part that changes most often.

For instance, a company's pricing rules are likely to change far more often than its order-to-cash process. If only the business process can be changed quickly then the company will not be able to respond to the far more numerous pricing changes without changing its process, an unnecessary step. Digital Decisioning allows an organization to control business processes through the critical decisions that support them. This increases the agility built into a process and allows for a stable process even when decision-making is constantly changing and evolving.

Explicitly identifying decisions and describing the logic behind them allows this logic to be managed and updated separately from the process itself, dramatically increasing the agility of an organization.

Digital Decisioning involves constant change to reflect new regulations, new policies and new conditions. In Digital Decisioning, change must be easy, it must be reliable, it must be fast, and it must be cost-effective.

Principle #3: Be Predictive Not Reactive

Organizations have spent heavily on Business Intelligence and Performance Management technology for managing, visualizing and analyzing data. These investments have been focused on analyzing the past and presenting this analysis to human users. They have relied, reasonably enough, on their human users to make extrapolations about the future. Users of these systems are making decisions based on this data, using what has happened in the past to guide how they will act in the future. Many of these systems can also bring users' attention to changes in data quickly to prompt decision-making. The value of this investment in terms of improved human decision-making is clear.

These approaches will not work for Digital Decisioning. When a decision is being automated, there is no human to do the extrapolation. Using only historical data in Digital Decisioning is like driving with only the rear-view mirror—every decision being made would be based on out-of-date and backward-looking data. In fact it would be worse, as a human driver can make guesses as to what's in front of them based on what they see in a rear view mirror. They will be reasonably accurate too, unless the road is changing direction quickly. Systems are not that smart. Digital Decisioning means supplying needed extrapolations explicitly. Without some view of the future and the likely impacts of different decision alternatives, opportunities and threats will not be identified in time to decide to do anything about them.

Predicting likely future behavior is at the core of using predictions in Digital Decisioning. You need to predict individual customer behavior such as how likely they are to default on a loan or respond to a particular offer. You need to predict if their behavior will be negative or positive in response to each possible action you could take, predicting how much additional revenue a customer might generate for each possible action. You want to know how likely it is that a transaction represents risky or fraudulent behavior. Ultimately, you want to be able to predict the best possible action to take based on everything you know, by considering the likely future behavior of a whole group of customers.

Digital Decisioning requires predictions to provide the context in which they can act rather than simply react to the data available at the time a decision is made. Digital Decisioning requires access to predictions that turn inherent uncertainty about the future into usable probabilities. You cannot know, for instance, which claims are definitely fraudulent—this is uncertain. You can embed a predictive analytic model developed using a machine learning or AI algorithm that predicts how likely it is that a specific claim is fraudulent.

There are three kinds of predictions relevant to Digital Decisioning: Analytic, Machine Learning or AI models that predict risk or fraud, that predict opportunity and that predict the impact of decisions. These predictions can direct, guide or push digital decision making in the right direction.

Predict Risk or Fraud

Most repeatable decisions do not have a huge economic impact individually. Despite their limited scope, many do have a significant gap between good and bad decisions. The value of the decision varies significantly with how well they are made. This gap arises when there is a risk of a real loss if a decision is made poorly. For instance, a well-judged loan offer to someone who will pay it back as agreed might net a bank a few tens of dollars in profit. A poorly judged offer will result in the loss of the loan principal—perhaps thousands of dollars. This mismatch between upside and downside is characteristic of risk-based decisions. Similarly, a poorly made decision in detecting fraud can result in large sums being transferred to an imposter or large purchases being made using stolen credit cards.

It is essential that Digital Decisioning be informed by an accurate assessment of the risks of the particular transaction or customer concerned. Such models might be focused on fraud, using analysis of patterns revealed in past fraudulent transactions to predict how likely it is that this transaction is also fraudulent. They might be focused on the likelihood of default, using a customer's past payment history and the history of other customers like them to predict how likely it is that they will fail to make payments in a timely fashion.

Many machine learning techniques can be used to build such models from historical data. Most require knowledge of which historical transactions were "bad"—fraudulent or in default. These known cases are used to train a model to predict how similar a new transaction is to these "bads." Unsupervised learning can also be used to find outliers when no labeled data exists. Once a prediction exists, it can be used in Digital Decisioning to treat those transactions or customers with particularly high or low risk differently.

Predict Opportunity

Many decisions do not involve an assessment of downside risk, but they still have some variability. Not driven entirely by compliance with regulations or policies, these decisions require an assessment of opportunity before an appropriate choice can be made. There is typically no absolute downside if a poor decision is made, simply a missed opportunity. Digital Decisioning requires insight to manage these tradeoffs.

These decisions are largely, though not exclusively, about how to treat customers. Deciding which offer to make to a customer or which ad to display to a visitor are examples of decisions where the "best" decision is one which makes the most of the opportunity to interact with the customer or visitor. Historical data can be used to predict how appealing a particular offer or product might be to a particular person or to a specific segment of customers. The value to the company of each offer, combined with the likelihood that a particular customer will accept it, can then be used to identify the most effective offer—to make the best decision.

When many such offers are being considered, it may be complex to identify the "best" offer. It may be difficult to manage the tradeoffs between the various decisions. In these circumstances, Digital Decisioning can take advantage of optimization technology that allows the tradeoffs to be explicitly defined and then the "optimal" or best outcome can be selected mathematically.

Predict Impact of Decisions

Sometimes the effect of an automated action cannot be precisely determined. For instance, the value of a subscription for a mobile phone will vary with the use made of the phone. When an action is available for a decision and has this kind of uncertainty about its value, a further prediction is needed.

The likely impact of each action on the profitability, risk or retention of a customer can be predicted by analyzing the behavior of other similar customers who were treated the same way—for whom the same action was taken. The prediction of the likely impact of each action can be combined with predictions of risk and opportunity to improve the quality of decision making in Digital Decisioning.

Principle #4: Test, Learn, Continuously Improve

Most information systems have a single approach to handling any decisions that have been embedded in them. Every transaction is treated the same way. Possible alternative approaches are eliminated during design to find the "best" approach. Information systems continue to work the way they were originally designed until someone explicitly re-codes them to behave differently. The only way these systems are changed is when a human decides that a change is required.

These systems also accumulate large amounts of data about customers, products, and other aspects of the business. This data might show that certain actions are more effective than others. Regardless, the system will continue with its programmed behavior. Every customer is treated like the first.

This approach is not an effective way to deliver Digital Decisioning. When we make decisions about our own lives or interactions, we often explicitly or implicitly assess a large amount of data. We learn from this data what is likely to work or not work. The data accumulated provides clues to how an effective decision can be made. Digital Decisioning cannot afford to ignore accumulated historical data about the effectiveness of decisions.

Decisions involve making a selection from a range of alternative actions and then taking the selected action. It is often not immediately obvious if the decision was made effectively. Some decisions have a significant time to outcome, and no assessment of the effectiveness of the decision will be possible until that time has passed. For instance, an early intervention designed to ensure a customer renews their annual contract cannot be assessed until the customer reaches the renewal point, perhaps many months later. If the action taken turns out to be ineffective, then a different approach will need to be considered. You cannot afford to "single thread" this analysis by only testing one decision making approach at a time.

Whether a decision is a good one or a bad one is a moving target. A decision may be made to discount a particular order for a customer that may be competitive today but much less so tomorrow because a competitor has changed their pricing. As markets, competitors, and consumer behavior shift, they affect the effectiveness of a decision. This constant change in the definition of an effective decision means you must continuously refine and improve your approach to Digital Decisioning.

Digital Decisioning therefore requires a rigorous approach to test, learn, and continuously improve results. The analysis and resulting changes may be made by human observers or by the system itself in a more automated fashion using continuous learning algorithms. Success in Digital Decisioning means collecting data about the effectiveness of decision making and using this data to refine and improve decision making approaches. Digital Decisioning often involves multiple potential decision-making approaches being tried simultaneously. These are continually compared to see which ones work and which ones do not. Successful ones persist and evolve, unsuccessful ones are jettisoned. Digital Decisioning must assume that decision-making will need to change and improve over time—that any approach will be imperfect when initially implemented but will be optimized as time passes. This analysis and improvement may be a manual process. The advent of machine learning is increasingly resulting in automated, continuous improvement.

Collect and Use Information to Improve

When a decision is automated, the decision made and why it was made must be recorded. This decision performance information allows the long-term effectiveness of a decision to be assessed. It can be integrated with the organization's performance metrics to see which decisions result in which positive, or negative, performance outcomes. This information allows good decisions to be differentiated from bad ones, better ones from worse ones. It is often said that if you wish to improve something, you must first measure it. Decisions are not an exception to this rule.

Information about the decisions made can and should be combined with the information used to make the decision. This information might be about a customer, a product, a claim, or other transaction. Combining this information with the decision performance information will identify differences in performance. These are caused by differences in the information used to drive the decision. For instance, a decision making approach may work well for customers with income below a certain level and poorly for those above it. Storing, integrating, analyzing, and using this data to improve decision making is the first building block in continuous improvement of Digital Decisioning.

Support Experimentation (Test and Learn)

When adopting Digital Decisioning, it may not be clear what approach will result in the best outcomes for the organization. Several alternative approaches might all be valid candidates for "best approach." Simulation and modeling of these approaches, and testing them against historical data, might show which approach is most likely to be superior. Even if the historical data points to a clear winner, the approach is going to be used against new data and may not perform as well in these circumstances.

Digital Decisioning often requires experiments, choosing between multiple defined approaches for real transactions. The approach used for each transaction can be recorded, and this information will allow the approaches to be compared to see which is superior. This comparison may not be definitive, and one approach may be better for some segments of a customer base, while a second works better for other segments. Results from these experiments can then be used to update with the most successful approach or combination of approaches. Because Digital Decisioning focuses on repeatable decisions, there will always be more decisions to be made that will be able to take advantage of this improved approach.

Optimize Over Time

In a static world, one round of experimentation might be enough to find the best approach. A set of experiments could be conducted and the most effective approach selected. As long as nothing changes, this approach will continue to be most effective. However, the effectiveness of a decision-making approach can vary over time for many reasons, and you have little or no control over this. The old "best" approach may degrade suddenly or gradually, and when it does, you will need to have alternatives. Even when experimentation finds a clear winner, therefore, Digital Decisioning requires that you keep experimenting to see if any of the alternative approaches have begun to outperform the previous winner. Alternative approaches could be those rejected as inferior initially or new ones developed specifically to see if a new approach would be superior in the changing circumstances. The effect of this continuous and never-ending experimentation is to optimize results over time by continually refining and improving decision-making approaches.

4. Delivering Digital Decisioning

Digital Decisioning is powerful. It applies the power of analytics and machine learning, gives business owners control and agility, and adapts and learns for continuous improvement. Companies using Digital Decisioning to deliver the value of AI need a proven approach to deliver Digital Decisioning.

Decision Management has been effectively applying the technologies of AI for more than a decade. As the technology has evolved, so has the approach - though the core elements have remained consistent. It is the effective, proven, reliable way to deliver digital decisioning you need.

Decision Management is much more than just the adoption of a set of AI technologies. Decision Management is a set of techniques and business capabilities that let you apply AI technologies such as business rules, machine learning and optimization to automate and manage your day to day operational decisions. It helps you focus on the design, creation, management and continuous improvement of digital decisioning assets.

Decision Management changes the way you apply technology in three broad areas:

- It adds techniques and tasks to explicitly identify and model your decisions.
- It combines the relevant set of AI technologies to automate each decision and deploys them as an integrated decision-making component—a Decision Service.
- It extends your performance management approach to include monitoring and improving decision-making itself based on logging, outcomes and experiments.

The next three chapters lay out the approach in three broad phases as shown in Figure 4-1.

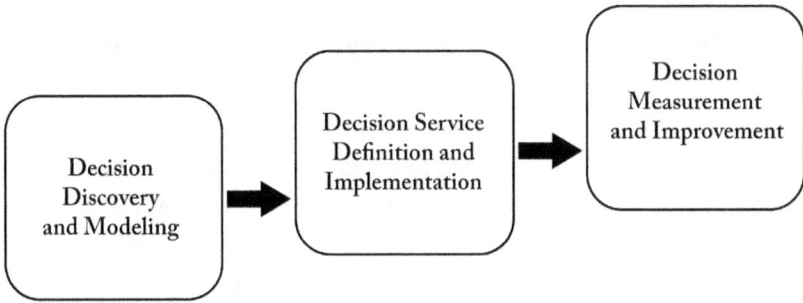

Figure 4-1 Decision Management Stages

1. Discover and Model Decisions

   Identify and describe the repeatable decisions that matter to a business—the ones that drive operational results. Define a decision model to capture a transparent, unambiguous definition of the decisions that are to be managed. Link decisions to performance measures and KPIs (Key Performance Indicators), so that it is clear what changes to decision-making will be required to improve any given measure. Document requirements for the different AI approaches that will be required to automate these decisions.

2. Build Decision Services

   Create Decision Services to automate some of the modeled decisions. Use the decision model to scope and specify these Decision Services. Use these stand-alone components to deliver the right mix of AI technologies into your systems and processes. They answer questions such as "how should we handle this claim?" or "what is the right discount for this order?" Decision models show how the various AI technologies used are being orchestrated to deliver the best answer.

3. Monitor and Improve Decisions

   Close the loop to ensure that decision-making is monitored and constantly improved to cope with a changing environment and deliver increasing value over time. With Decision Management, the business understands how specific decisions create value. Monitor decision performance so business owners understand and manage their decisions more effectively by targeting improvements.

5.Discover and Model Decisions

The most fundamental of the four principles of Digital Decisioning is the first—begin with the decision in mind. Digital Decisioning is focused on automating and improving specific decisions. Digital Decisioning is not about executing complete business processes. It is focused on providing decision-making to allow processes to execute more effectively or to run straight through without manual intervention. Digital Decisioning does not replace complete legacy systems, just the hard to change decision-making components.

To implement Digital Decisioning, we must know what decisions are involved. We must identify appropriate decisions, then document, design, and understand them. Existing software approaches do not focus on decisions at this level of detail.

The first phase of Decision Management as shown in Figure 5-1 is to Discover and Model decisions that will repay an investment in Digital Decisioning.

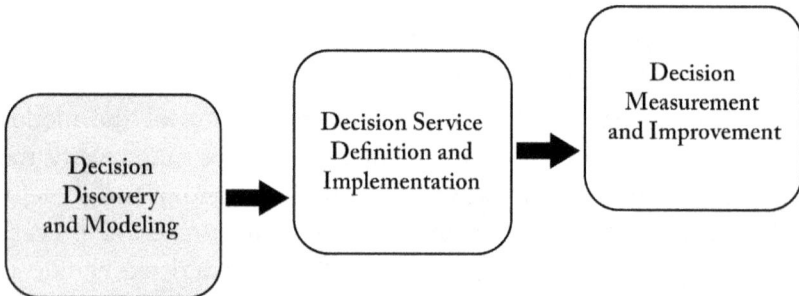

Figure 5-1 Decision Discovery and Modeling in Context

Characteristics of Suitable Decisions

Organizations make many decisions of many different types. Not all these decisions are suitable for automation. Before using Decision Management and automating a specific decision, it is important to be sure it has suitable characteristics. Suitable decisions are repeatable, non-trivial, and measurable. The organization must also be able to accept automation for the decision so you don't end up with an automated decision that no-one uses.

Repeatable

By far the most important criterion for a suitable decision is repeatability. If a decision is not repeatable then there is no value in automating it. To be considered repeatable a decision must pass four tests:

1. It is possible to say when the decision will need to be made.

2. Each time the decision is made the same information is available, considered and analyzed.

3. The set of possible actions remains consistent between decisions.

4. The way in which the success of these actions is measured in terms of business outcomes remains consistent.

For example, the decision about which cross sell offer to make to a customer at checkout passes all four tests:

1. The decision is made every time a customer checks out with a new order.

2. The customer profile, their past orders, and their current order are analyzed to determine the most appropriate cross-sell.

3. The cross sell is always a product selected from the current catalog.

4. Success is defined as an increase in the value of a customer order after the cross-sell offer is made relative to the value of that order before the cross-sell offer was made.

Note that the content of the information in steps 2 and 3 change from decision to decision, but the structure or scope of the information does not.

The Decision Is Made at Defined Times

An organization knows when a repeatable decision must be made. Such a decision might be made for all transactions of a certain type. A decision might be required for a process to complete or move to the next step, allowing an organization to define it in terms of a process context. For instance, decisions about claim validity are made for every submitted claim. In more event-centric environments, a decision might be required when a specific event is received. For instance, a pattern of sensor events might identify a piece of hardware as being close to failure, and a decision must then be made regarding which engineer to dispatch to look at it. Finally, a decision may be made on a regular schedule such as hourly, daily, or weekly. For instance, a bank may check to see if it has wealth management recommendations for its best customers every week. The need to make these decisions is knowable in advance.

It is also possible to know that a decision must be made many times in the course of a year without knowing exactly when such a decision will need to be made. These decisions may be made in response to some external driver over which the organization has no control, such as competitive changes or the weather. Decisions may also be proactive, driven by considerations of individuals not knowable to the organization's systems. These decisions may still be repeatable if the organization can define the circumstances in which a decision will be made. For example, an outbound marketing campaign may launch based on a wide range of factors, but if the organization knows it will decide to launch an outbound campaign multiple times each month and can articulate the circumstances in which it will do so (competitor launches a new product or changes pricing, news item is relevant to a product, etc.), then this decision can pass the test for being made at defined times as the organization knows what the conditions are that will trigger the need for a decision.

The Same Information Is Used Each Time

The second test for repeatability is information. For a decision to be repeatable it must use a consistent set of information. This will allow the implementation of an interface to pull this information into the system when the decision is automated. The corollary of this is that a consistent set of information must be available each time the decision is made.

This does not mean that every time the decision is made an identical set of information is presented to it. It does mean, however, that a set of information can be defined that is a superset of the information that will be presented each time.

For example, a decision about a customer retention offer will use the customer's profile and the products they have purchased as part of its decision-making. This is consistent from decision to decision, although the completeness of a customer profile and the number of products owned by a customer will vary from customer to customer. The specific information about a customer and their products will differ each time

64

but the basic structure of the information will remain consistent. This decision about a customer retention offer could only be made when this information was available.

Avoid Information Supersets

The intent of this test is not to define a massive superset of information to link disparate decisions into a set. If it is not possible to define a coherent set of information that is used repeatedly then the decision will not pass this test.

Defined Set of Actions

A decision always selects from a set of possible or allowed actions. These might be a list of customer treatments, loan terms, offers, or products. They might also be a range of values such as a price or discount level. The act of making a decision selects one or more of these possible actions. Repeatable decisions have the same set of actions each time. Different actions will be selected each time the decision is made, but the set of actions remains consistent between decisions. For instance, each loan originated will make different selections of the appropriate terms and prices based on the specifics of the loan application. Nevertheless, the set of possible terms and prices is the same for each decision.

Decisions change over time

This test for repeatability does not mean that the allowed actions for a decision do not vary over time. Decision making is dynamic and new possible actions may be defined and existing ones "retired" as the decision-making approach is refined. This kind of evolution does not mean that a decision is not repeatable. A repeatable decision is one in which the same actions are available each time a decision is made between such changes in the decision-making approach.

Consistent Measurement of Success

The final test for repeatability is that good and bad decisions can be consistently identified. Nothing can be improved if it cannot be measured, and decision-making is no exception. It is essential to understand how to measure the success of each decision in terms of outcomes that make sense of the business. This is true of all decisions, even one-off ad-hoc decisions. For repeatable decisions, the measurement of success is consistent over time. For example, a decision about which supplier to use for a particular part is measured by assessing on-time delivery and by counting any quality problems with the supply. This assessment is consistent for every supplier selection decision.

Non-Trivial

The second test for a suitable decision is that it is non-trivial. Digital Decisioning represents an investment of time and money. Organizations will only a see a return on this investment if the decision being automated is one that is non-trivial and has a degree of complexity. The drivers of this complexity are:

- Policies and regulations.
- The need for domain knowledge.
- The need to analyze large data volumes or complex data.
- The need to select from very large numbers of possible outcomes.
- The need to trade-off competing objectives.
- The need to update the decision-making approach often.

Non-trivial decisions do not need to pass all of these tests. Very complex regulations or very difficult tradeoffs might be enough to classify a decision as non-trivial regardless of other factors. However, no one test need be very severe if a decision has elements of several. A decision based on a few policies, some straightforward analysis, and a simple trade-off may be non-trivial thanks to the combination of factors.

Policies and Regulations

Perhaps the most common drivers of complexity in repeatable decisions are the existence of policies and regulations that must be followed when deciding. Organizations often have policies that constrain decision making to ensure consistency and to avoid known problems or pitfalls. For instance, organizations may have policies that define the minimum size of companies who can act as suppliers of critical parts or that insist on specific terms being included in loans above a certain size. Ensuring that decisions made are always compliant with these policies can be complex.

Many decisions an organization makes are also constrained by regulations, particularly when those decisions relate to individual consumers or to interactions with government agencies. For instance, the ways in which companies decide who gets credit is heavily regulated to prevent bias, while other regulations control exactly what kinds of medical services the government will pay for. Organizations want to be sure they follow these regulations when making decisions as the consequences of not doing so can include fines, rejected payment requests, and even legal action. Increasingly governments are insisting that organizations not only comply with these regulations but *demonstrate* that they are complying with these regulations. This need for execution transparency can make even straightforward regulations a driver for Digital Decisioning.

Domain Knowledge and Expertise

Some decisions are hard to make the first time you try. More experience making the decision often makes it easier to make the decision quickly and increases the chances that you will make a good decision. For instance, deciding on the cause of a problem in a piece of machinery is hard when you are unfamiliar with the machinery and how to debug it. As you gain experience the decision becomes easier, and you are more likely to correctly identify the root cause of a problem. Decisions like these require domain knowledge and expertise. Some require relatively little domain knowledge, the kind that can be acquired in a few days by watching an experienced operator. Others require years of experience or extensive mentoring to build a suitable level of expertise. These kinds of decisions are non-trivial as making a good one requires deep understanding of a domain.

Analysis Is Required

While some decisions can be made solely by following the policies or regulations defined for the decision, many require some analysis. If a decision involves making the "best" or "most appropriate" selection, then some judgment or analysis is going to be needed. The decision can be made only once the information available is considered and analyzed. This need for analysis does not mean the decision is not repeatable, or automatable, just that it is a somewhat more complex decision. Repeatable and well-defined analysis can be part of a decision without requiring manual decision-making as long as the analysis can be defined in advance.

Several kinds of analysis are possible. The analysis might be to categorize someone or something so that a decision can be made based on that categorization. For instance, someone's driving history might be analyzed to see which risk segment they should be put into when underwriting an auto policy for them. Analysis might result in an assessment of risk, fraud, or opportunity. For instance, a business might be analyzed to see how likely they are to pay back a commercial loan. Analysis might also assess a propensity or likelihood. For instance, the propensity of a customer to buy a specific product might be needed before deciding which product to offer.

The analysis can be of the current information—such as all the data in an application or an order—or of historical information—such as all the prior transactions of a customer. A requirement for either kind of analysis shows a decision is non-trivial.

Large Amounts of Data

Some decisions involve the consideration of large amounts of data. When the values of large numbers of data elements must be considered to make a decision then it is likely to be non-trivial. For instance, a decision to approve an application for a complex loan product may be non-trivial simply because the application contains hundreds of data elements that must be validated and cross-checked.

Large Numbers of Actions

A decision that requires selection from a small number of possible actions is generally simpler than one requiring selection from many possible actions. As the number of possible actions rises, so does the likelihood that a decision is going to be non-trivial. It is often said that people have a hard time with lists containing more than seven or so items. Any decision that involves selecting from more options than this is likely to be complex enough to be a good candidate for Digital Decisioning.

Of course, a decision can be extremely complex and still only have a couple of possible actions. The underwriting of a complex commercial development project may only have two actions—yes or no—and yet remain an extremely difficult decision to make. Still, a large number of possible actions makes a decision more complex.

Trade-offs Must Be Made

Many decisions involve trade-offs. These decisions are selecting from possible outcomes, none of which is "perfect." Either each outcome has potential downsides that must be balanced against potential upsides, or each outcome has downstream consequences that must be balanced against their value. For instance, a sourcing decision may have to consider both the price a new supplier is offering and the impact the order would have on cumulative discounts from existing suppliers. Some trade-offs are extremely straightforward and easy to make, others are much more complex. Sometimes there is an optimal or best trade off, but often there is only a need for a reasonable one. The need to make a trade-off almost always means that a decision is a non-trivial one.

Regular Updates

Even if a decision appears trivial using all the previous criteria, the need for regular updates to the decision-making approach may be enough to make the decision non-trivial. Some decisions have a stable decision-making approach that does not change very much over time. New regulations or policies may be issued once a year, for instance. Sometimes the decision-making approach must change much more often. Regularly scheduled monthly, weekly, or daily changes are not uncommon in decision-making. For instance, pricing guidelines for heavily traded products might change every day while new fraud detection approaches could be released every week. Such regular updates can easily justify considering a decision non-trivial.

In addition to regularly scheduled changes, some decisions have a need for regular but less predictable updates. For instance, some fraud rules are not released on a regular schedule but must be updated rapidly once identified. Decisions that have a need for immediate updates, even if those updates are rare, are generally non-trivial.

Measurable Business Impact

It must be possible to show a return on your investment in Digital

Decisioning. Repeatable decisions are more likely to show this return as there are many decisions to make in the future that will be made automatically thanks to your investments. Similarly, non-trivial decisions are more likely to show a return, as their complexity means that relying on less well-defined decision-making approaches is likely to result in poorer quality decisions.

A suitable decision also needs to have a definable and measurable business impact. It must be possible to see the cost of bad decisions and the value of good ones. For a suitable decision, the organization can see the impact of a decision in terms that relate to the measurement framework the organization already has. If an organization values customer loyalty, then the business impact of a customer retention decision could be measured in terms of an increase in customer loyalty. If an organization focuses on being a low-cost provider, then decisions could be measured in terms of their ability to reduce costs. A suitable decision has a defined, observable and measurable impact on the organization.

Begin with measurement infrastructure

It is sometimes possible to see that a decision is important to the business, and perhaps to understand what impact it has, without being able to measure that impact. Experience suggests that it is best to begin by creating the infrastructure that will allow the measurement of the impact before automating and improving the decision.

This measurement infrastructure should capture and report on the right data to assess decision effectiveness. This includes being able to track what actions were taken as a result of a decision and being able to link future outcomes back to these actions.

The business impact of a decision may not be immediately apparent. It can take months or even years to see the total impact of improving how a decision is made. Improving the initial product configuration decision for a subscription product may improve long term customer retention, but this won't be apparent until the customers affected by the improved decision reach their annual renewal point.

It may also be difficult to measure the impact of a single decision. It is not reasonable, for instance, to consider the improvement in portfolio risk caused by a single loan origination decision. An improvement in the quality of loan origination decisions will, however, show a cumulative improvement in portfolio risk over time.

Candidates for Automation

There is one final test for suitable decisions. If a decision is repeatable, non-trivial, and has a measurable business impact, it will not be suitable unless the organization accepts it as a candidate for automation. There is no value to creating a system that is not used. If the decision is one that the organization fundamentally believes requires human judgment, then it is not a suitable decision.

> **Suitability changes over time**
>
> This is not as simple a test as it appears. The way organizations think about decisions and decision-making evolves. The expectations of younger workers who grew up with computers are different from those who began work with manual processes. Industry norms change over time as proof points from early adopters become widely known. Corporate cultures that hold automation back can be changed or overridden with enough of a crisis. Observing how a decision is made manually can show that an automated decision would be better and build enthusiasm for it. Just because a decision is not a good candidate today does not mean that it will not become one in the future.

Decision models decompose a decision into a set of simpler decisions on which the main decision is dependent. The top-level decision may not be a candidate because the organization is unwilling to have a machine make that decision. Lower-level decisions, however, may be suitable simply because the more limited scope of those decisions makes an organization more comfortable with having a computerized approach. Similarly, a model of decision-making might show how decisions made by humans can be fitted into a broader, automated framework, reassuring the organization that the role of human judgment will be sustained. For instance, a large commercial underwriting decision may be one that an insurer does not consider a candidate for automation. In this case, an underwriter is going to be charged with making the decision. The organization might be comfortable automating some elements of this decision, such as selecting the right terms for the kind of project or identifying the amount of reinsurance required.

A Decision Taxonomy

Many decisions made by an organization are suitable for Digital Decisioning. Decisions that have suitable characteristics fall into several distinct categories. Decisions in each of these categories have a distinct style or profile. Understanding these profiles can help in identifying and describing decisions. The most common categories are eligibility, validation, calculation, risk, fraud, opportunity and micro decisions.

Eligibility

Many decisions are about determining eligibility. Products and services cannot always be sold to every customer. Government benefits are not payable to all citizens. Not every organization can bid on certain kinds of contract. Determining if a person or organization is eligible is a decision.

Eligibility decisions are often good candidates for Digital Decisioning. They are highly repeatable as every person or organization that applies should be assessed the same way. Outcomes are well defined—typically only "Yes" and "No with reasons." The information available to make the decision is both consistent and well defined. Eligibility decisions typically have a very fixed approach with little room for judgment as they are heavily regulated or constrained by policy.

An example would be a decision regarding banking products that might be offered to a customer. Offering a product as a cross-sell that the customer is not eligible for will result in poor customer service. A decision about the products a customer is eligible for is required. Based on information known about a customer, regulations that prohibit certain products in certain states, minimum age requirements, and the bank's policies for each product, it is possible to determine which products should be considered for cross-selling.

Validation

Very similar to eligibility decisions, validations are well-defined and highly repeatable decisions. These decisions are typically used as gates controlling sequence or process. Until or unless the transaction or customer can be validated the process cannot continue. Validation decisions are mostly driven by policies, though these policies can come from outside the organization such as an industry standards body.

For example, a claim may be validated before processing. This ensures that the claim contains a complete set of information and that basic checks such as a valid address have been performed before more time consuming and complex tasks are scheduled.

Calculation

Calculation decisions are often missed in the identification of suitable decisions. It is easy to think of calculations as completely fixed and therefore trivial in the context of Digital Decisioning. However, some calculations are based on policies that change regularly, and some are more specific to a customer than might at first appear to be the case. Rather than asking, "what is the price for this product" and regarding this as a trivial look up in a database, it can be more informative to ask, "what is the correct price for this product for this person at this time?" Such a calculation is clearly a non-trivial decision with opportunities to personalize the pricing or have it reflect rapidly changing demand or competitive environments.

Risk Decisions

While calculation, eligibility, and validation decisions are driven by policies and regulations, risk decisions are driven by the need to assess how risky a customer or transaction is. The potential for a significant loss drives the need for risk assessment. These decisions have a large gap between the value of a good decision and the value of a bad one. For instance, when a loan is offered to someone, there is a risk that they will not repay the loan. If the loan is not repaid, then the lender suffers a significant financial loss. If the loan is repaid, then the lender gains financially from the interest paid. The upside potential of such a decision is typically significantly less than the downside risk. A good loan might result in tens or hundreds of dollars in fees, while a bad one might result in a multi-thousand dollar write off. This large difference between the upside and the downside of a risk decision is its defining characteristic.

Managing portfolio risk is not enough

When many organizations think about risk decisions they often focus on portfolio-level risk decisions. For instance, deciding on a sub-prime lending strategy to manage their exposure to high risk but profitable loans. While these are important risk decisions, the kind of repeatable decision we are discussing is more important. Organizations do not generally acquire risk in large lumps but one transaction, one loan, one customer at a time. Deciding on the terms for a specific sub-prime loan is the decision that must be made correctly if the portfolio is not to become unbalanced. The portfolio decision constrains this repeatable decision but it is the repeatable decision that prevents bad loans from entering the portfolio in the first place.

There are often policies and regulations that must be applied in a risk decision. These might constrain the decision or define how the risk assessment itself can be made. Risks can be assessed judgmentally, using experts as a source. Predictive analytics and machine learning are widely used to assess risk using historical data. A data-driven approach is generally to be preferred whenever possible. The use of predictive analytic and machine learning models to predict how risky a particular transaction or customer is likely to be is at the heart of risk decisions. Most organizations need to be able to explain risk decisions after the fact.

As a result, only explicable models that clearly show what is driving the prediction will be acceptable. In addition, organizations will want to be able to show causation in these models — that the drivers of these models have some clear link to the riskiness of behavior.

Fraud Decisions

Fraud and abuse decisions are those where the action to be taken is dependent on whether the transaction or customer is other than they seem. Examples include a decision if the customer is who they say they are or that this claim is for a medical procedure that has genuinely been carried out. While fraud is deliberate, many situations where the system is being abused or where there is a failure to follow best practices look like fraudulent transactions because they fall outside the norms. Considering fraud and abuse a single category can therefore be helpful as the approaches are often similar.

Fraud decisions are very similar to risk decisions in that there is a large downside if a decision is made poorly. The risk of fraud is also likely to be assessed with an analytic or machine learning model. These decisions are a different category for two reasons:

- First, when detecting fraud and abuse, there is generally less need to be able to explain the predictions involved. Providing they work well and predict a lot of "bad" transactions accurately while mislabeling only a small number of "good" ones, they are acceptable. This means that more powerful but opaque forms of machine learning such as neural networks can be used.

- Second there is a difference in volatility. Risk decisions involve regulations (especially where the decision is about consumers) and long-term risk-management policies that do not change all that often. Fraud decisions involve policies that are based on the changing behavior of fraudsters, tips from law enforcement, and other highly volatile sources.

For these reasons it is worth considering fraud and abuse decisions as being distinct from risk decisions.

Opportunity Decisions

Some decisions are only lightly constrained by policies and regulations. If the decision has little or no possible downside no risk assessment is required. The key driver for such a decision will be an assessment of opportunity. The potential value of each possible action that could be taken will be used to select between them. Opportunity decisions often ask how profitable might this customer be if we take one of the possible actions?

Opportunity decisions are generally those that are customer-centric such as cross-sell and up-sell decisions. Opportunity decisions also use expert judgment, and increasingly, analytics or machine learning to predict the likely response of a customer and the potential size of the opportunity. It is also common for opportunity decisions to have to change rapidly to take advantage of competitive and market circumstances. Many use optimization to find the "best" opportunity.

Some opportunity decisions do not relate to customers. It is possible to assess the opportunity for future discounts from a supplier as part of selecting a supplier or to consider the opportunity value of different ways to use a spare asset.

Opportunity decisions are different

Because there is often little difference between good and bad opportunity decisions it is helpful to think of these as separate from risk decisions and fraud decisions. It is not helpful to simply "reverse" how you look at an opportunity to make money and consider it a risk that you will not make any money. The kind of analysis you do when trying to avoid a loss is different from the kind you do when you are examining two alternatives to see which will benefit you the most.

Micro Decisions

When searching for repeatable operational decisions it is important to consider how fine grained a decision you are really making. Often what appears to be a single decision is many "micro decisions" (Taylor & Raden, 2007). A micro decision is a decision from a customer's perspective. For instance, when a consumer receives a piece of direct mail they respond as though that piece of mail was sent just to them. If it is not relevant, then they class it as "junk" and downgrade their opinion of the company that sent it (especially if they are already a customer of that company).

76

The customer's perspective is typically not shared by the company. The marketing department of this company probably thinks they made a single decision to send an offer to everyone in a customer segment—10,000 or 100,000 pieces of mail from a single decision. When evaluating this marketing decision to see if it is a suitable decision for Digital Decisioning, it is much more informative to consider the micro decision perspective. There is no particular reason why the company could not make a different decision for each letter. It could generate a letter for James, a letter for Erick, a letter for Jean. It could treat each letter as a micro decision. This micro decision could be automated to generate a targeted, intensely personalized letter for each of the 10,000 or 100,000 customers. As long as the marketing decision is thought of as a single decision for all the letters, this kind of 1:1 marketing will not be possible.

Most micro decisions are about customers, though there are often analogous decisions for suppliers, agents, employees and partners. Micro decisions can be risk or opportunity decisions, though most missed micro decisions are opportunity decisions.

Repeatable Management Decisions

Calculations; eligibility and validation decisions; risk, fraud and opportunity decisions are all operational decisions. Operational decisions make up the majority of suitable decisions for Digital Decisioning, but not all. Some suitable repeatable decisions are tactical decisions. A planning decision that is made every day or a decision about budgeting for customer retention might be examples of tactical decisions that are repeatable.

These decisions are not going to be as repeatable as operational decisions and are likely to involve more degrees of freedom for the decision-maker. They are likely to be made by a knowledge worker or manager with the skills and know-how to use business intelligence tools and spreadsheets. The application of Digital Decisioning in these decisions is likely to be one of supporting a decision maker or integrating a human decision-maker into an automated frame rather than one of trying to completely automate the decision. For instance, you might constrain the available outcomes so that the decision maker can focus on only those that are valid, given company policy and risk models. Alternatively, the automation might assemble the right subset of the available information and present it to the decision maker so that they focus on the highest risk elements of the decision. Their input can then be integrated back into an automated outcome. It can be helpful to think of the resulting system as a blend of traditional decision support with Digital Decisioning.

Finding Suitable Decisions

Organizations of even quite modest size make many decisions that are suitable for automation. Repeatable, non-trivial, and measurable decisions of many different types are widespread. However, most organizations have never attempted to inventory these decisions. As a result, it is hard to begin a Digital Decisioning initiative without first engaging in an exercise to find an appropriate set of decisions.

There are several ways to find suitable decisions including:

- A top-down approach.
- Process-centric analysis.
- Using an organization's metrics and key performance indicators (KPIs).
- Analyzing legacy systems.
- Event-centric analysis.

All these approaches have value, and most decision inventories are built using multiple approaches. Using several approaches cross-checks and validates the decisions and engages different people in the discussion, reducing the likelihood that a decision will be missed.

The objective of applying these various approaches is to develop a complete decision inventory. It is not a good idea to try and develop an organization-wide decision inventory as a single exercise. Like most such horizontal efforts, you are likely to become bogged down and spend far too long without showing a return on the time invested. Instead, focus on a specific area of the business or a small, tightly coupled set of business processes. Focus on the decisions within this area that make a difference to a goal or objective that you can measure. Once you have a first version of a decision inventory for this area of the business, invest in some high-ROI Digital Decisioning to prove out the approach. Iteration and incremental development of a decision inventory over time are critical to success with Digital Decisioning.

> **Projects focused on a specific decision**
>
> Many projects are focused on a specific decision from the very beginning. A project to automate claims handling or to make a suitable offer to a customer has already identified the decision that must be automated. For such projects, the focus is on finding sub-decisions and decomposing the decision not on developing a broad decision inventory. Many of the same techniques can be applied but the scope should be limited to those directly relevant to the project.

Top-down

Perhaps the most obvious, though not necessarily the easiest, way to find decisions is simply to brainstorm them. Working with a group of executives and decision-makers, start making lists of decisions made. Most of these decisions will not be suitable as they will not be sufficiently constrained or repeatable. Focus on the day-to-day decisions that implement the executive decisions identified as well as drawing out the hidden micro decisions behind these decisions; this will start to identify more and better candidates.

With an executive audience, it is also helpful to ask them what decisions their staff makes and to ask them about the exceptions the executives handle. Anything referred up the management chain is likely to be an example of a decision that is mostly made at a lower level in the organization. For instance, a risk officer who talks about handling approvals for really complex commercial loans is telling you that all commercial loans must be approved and that this happens somewhere further down the organization.

You can also ask executives about customer complaints. What decision or set of decisions provoked the customer's unhappiness? How about service outages or major company crises? Often these were triggered by a series of bad decisions, and executives are happy to tell you what decisions were involved.

A top-down approach is often very informative but rarely enough. Only in the most decision-centric industries (consumer credit cards or property and casualty insurance perhaps) will facilitated sessions and interviews of executives get you a reasonably complete decision inventory. A focus on the business processes in the area you have selected is likely to be essential.

The top down approach and executive goals

One of the key issues in any project is getting funding. A top-down approach has the advantage that it clearly begins with the things that matter to executives, with their goals and objectives. Any decisions identified will therefore be linked to and clearly supportive of these goals. This strong connection between the decisions found and the organization's strategic goals will help make the case for funding and help deliver strong executive sponsorship.

Process-centric

One of the best ways to find suitable decisions is by analyzing existing process designs. By and large, processes are only designed and automated if they are themselves repeatable. These processes are about the day-to-day operations of the organization, and as such, almost any decision that is relevant to these processes will also be a suitable, repeatable decision.

Most processes have been designed without an explicit focus on decisions. Decisions will therefore be hidden in the process design. Four approaches can be used separately or in combination to find the decisions in a process:

- Looking for explicit decision points.
- Evaluating similar processes.
- Looking at local exceptions.
- Examining every escalation or referral step.

Explicit Decision Points

Some processes have explicit decision points embedded in them. Decision points have two characteristics. First, there is a task in the process that is immediately followed by a branch or gateway that uses the result of that task to send the process down one of several paths. Second, this task typically uses a decisioning word in its name. For instance:

- **Determine** if someone is eligible for a benefit
- **Validate** the completeness of an invoice
- **Calculate** the discount for an order
- **Assess** the risk of a transaction
- **Select** the terms for a deal
- **Choose** which claims to Fast Track

Determine, validate, calculate, assess, select, and *choose* are all decisioning words. Any such decision point should be immediately identified and added to the decision inventory.

Gateway nests

Some process models have decision-making explicitly encoded in gateways. Gateways will be followed by other gateways or by tasks that simply retrieve more data required by subsequent gateways. The process map resembles a rail yard, full of complex branching and re-branching. Removing this branching and replacing it with an explicit decision point task will simplify the process, often dramatically. The nest of gateways will generally be much simpler to represent as a decision model.

Multiple Similar Processes

Once the explicit decision points have been documented, it is worth looking at the process inventory to see if there are groups or clusters of similar processes. Often these similar processes have a decision that is different, while everything else in the process is the same. Because the decision-making has been embedded in the process design, however, the processes all look different. For instance, a government agency might have multiple permit issuing processes or a financial institution might have different processes to record different transaction types. These processes are different because the criteria for each permit or transaction type are different. If checking these criteria is handled with process steps, then the processes will look quite different.

When multiple similar processes are found, look for a decision that is being made as part of the process. It is likely to be made slightly differently in each case, but often can be reduced to a single decision—such as "is company eligible for this permit" or "can this customer execute this transaction type on this account"—that is common across all the processes. Visual inspection of the processes can be used to confirm how similar the processes would be if the decision were to be externalized from the process.

Local Exceptions

Another common consequence of not identifying and managing decisions is a process with large numbers of local exceptions. These have often made what at first seemed to be a straightforward process look very complex. Each country, division, or product group might have defined its own exceptions to the global standard process that everyone is using. For example, a standard supplier onboarding process might be overloaded with hundreds of local exceptions to handle country-by-country requirements for supplier information.

It is often possible to define a decision that applies these local exceptions. Then everyone can use the standard process. For instance, the decision "do we have enough information about this supplier" could be defined. If that decision included country-specific guidance, everyone could use it. With access to such a decision, every group can use the standard process as all the exceptions to the process were really a way to capture how this decision should be made in each case. Identifying and externalizing the decision will simplify the process.

Escalation and Referral

The final sources of decisions in a process are manual escalations and referral tasks. When a process must sometimes stop while an issue with a transaction or question about a customer is escalated, a decision is involved. Generally, the person executing the process (such as a call center representative) is not considered sufficiently senior or well trained to make the decision, so it is escalated. These decisions are almost always good Digital Decisioning candidates.

Similarly, any time a process pauses while work is put on a worklist so that a human can be brought into the process, a decision is implied. Sometimes a human is brought in to apply their judgment or to interact with the real world in some way. A mortgage process might assign someone to go and inspect a property to decide what condition it is in.

These decisions are unlikely to be suitable for Digital Decisioning as they involve the physical world. Often little or no judgment is required and there is little freedom of action for the person assigned. They are expected to apply policies, regulations, or guidelines from a cheat sheet to make the decision and then push the transaction back into the process. These decisions are almost always good Digital Decisioning candidates.

Externalizing these decisions will not generally make a process simpler. The escalation or referral will still be required for those decisions that cannot be automated (yet). Digital Decisioning will make more transactions run straight through and improve throughput and efficiency.

Using Metrics and Performance Management Systems

The effectiveness with which decisions are made has a direct impact on business outcomes measured using key performance indicators (KPIs) and associated metrics. For example, missing fraud in claims processing results in the payment of fraudulent claims and losses that are hard to recover. Such a failure will be reflected in the various KPIs that monitor claims effectiveness. The number of "likely frauds" measured through post-analysis and the loss ratio will rise. An ineffective decision that identifies too many false positives results in unnecessary delay, increased overhead and poor customer satisfaction. All reflected in other KPIs and metrics.

Understanding the key decisions that are responsible for the business outcomes being monitored with KPIs and other metrics helps differentiate good decisions from bad ones. It shows which decisions to focus on when metrics or KPIs are out of acceptable bounds. An existing performance management environment can be used to identify decisions in several ways:

- Simple mapping of decisions and KPIs
- Analysis of past data
- Root cause analysis.

Mapping Decisions and KPIs

One of the simplest ways to find decisions using KPIs and metrics in a performance management system is simply to map them to the decisions found to date. If the top-level decisions identified are listed on the vertical axis of a table and the KPIs and metrics for the business are listed on the horizontal axis, an empty table is created. Each decision can be examined to see if it impacts each KPI or metric. A decision impacts a metric if a change in the quality of decision-making would move the metric. These relationships can be direct (where every change in decision-making shows up clearly in the metric) or indirect. In addition, they can be correlated (where improvement in the decision improves the metric) or inversely correlated (where improvement in the decision makes the metric worse). For instance, improving a customer retention decision might improve the retention metric, while "damaging" the retention budget metric.

Once the existing decisions have been analyzed, it is interesting to examine the gaps. Metrics and KPIs that have no decisions should be examined and discussed to see if there are decisions that have not yet been identified. It is possible for something to be monitored even though no decisions are made that impacts it, but it is unlikely. Similarly, decisions, that do not impact a metric may need to be examined in more detail. It may simply be that a metric is missing, but it may also be that the decision is poorly understood or impacts metrics and KPIs in other business units.

Analysis of Past Data

KPIs, whether mapped to decisions or not, can be analyzed over time for additional insight. The historical values of KPIs can reveal periods when the values were particularly good or particularly poor. Analysis of these values can also show inflexion points where something changed and significantly altered the trajectory of the KPI. If a structured approach to KPIs has been taken, then variation of KPIs between regions, teams, shifts or organizations may be identified.

Any of these variations in KPIs might be indicative of a decision that should be added to the inventory. When a period shows particularly good or bad results then it may well be that some decision was being made differently during this period. Discussing the period with those involved might reveal some initiative or change that is thought to be responsible. If the current decision inventory does not contain any decisions that would have been impacted by this initiative, then there may well another decision or set of decisions that can be identified —

those that were impacted by the initiative.

When there is a variation between organizations the likelihood is that these organizations make some decision or decisions differently. Analysis of the decisions already identified might make it clear where this variation exists. If none of the decisions identified so far vary between the organizations then an additional decision can be identified. Any additional decisions identified in this way should be associated with the relevant KPIs.

Root Cause Analysis

Some changes in the external environment cannot be addressed simply by improving or optimizing operational decisions. Sometimes a larger set of changes to business operations may be necessary to support a realigned business strategy as your organization responds to the changed business environment. For instance, you may have to restructure claims processing to introduce early fraud detection to counteract a rise in certain types of fraudulent claims. A new operational decision—"likely fraud"— has to be performed for each claim transaction. One of the most effective ways to discover the need for this kind of change is to perform root cause analysis on key performance indicators.

Analysis of key performance indicator data over time combined with drill-down analysis of associated data can provide insight into the underlying root causes. Detailed analysis of a "Time to Process" KPI might show that while the average is satisfactory there is a growing problem with occasional long delays for some loan applications. The delays might be observed as outliers in an aggregate completion time report. Further analysis can drill down to see what is causing these delays. The delay may come when all the necessary documentation is not collected before routing the application to a loan approver. The solution may be a change in the process to generate a checklist and ensuring all documents are collected before the loan approver gets involved. Implementing this involves a change to the process but also identifies a new decision—what is the correct checklist for this application?

> **What-if analysis of alternatives**
>
> With this kind of analysis, you can often come up with many alternative proposals to address a specific root cause. Not all changes will be equally effective and business modeling and simulation through "what if" analysis is essential to select a feasible and optimal approach. Considering the decisions that each approach would require and the degree to which those decisions might be automatable will help ensure the best choice.

Analyzing Legacy Systems

Some suitable decisions may already be automated in legacy systems. Legacy systems do not handle decisions well. Legacy systems are neither agile nor transparent. They were rarely designed with an explicit focus on decision-making. In very high throughput scenarios, however, some decisions may have been embedded in legacy code. When building a decision inventory, it may be useful to identify those parts of a legacy system that automate decisions. The two best signs of this are large numbers of change requests and table-driven code.

High Change Components

Decisions are high change elements of the business. Anytime there is a legacy module that is the subject of constant change requests, especially when these change requests come at regular intervals, there is a strong likelihood that the module is implementing a decision or decisions. For instance, if a regulated decision is implemented in code, then each time new regulations are issued, many change requests will likely be generated. IT will gradually work through these but will often get behind.

To find these decisions, use an application portfolio analysis tool if you have one, or review the change request and project logs to see where the efforts are focused. Examine these modules to see what they do and why they are being changed. If policy or regulatory change is the main driver, or if a business unit just needs the changes made to stay competitive, you will likely be able to describe a decision that is implemented by the module.

Table-driven Code

Because code is hard to change and because decisions are high change components, IT departments will sometimes attempt to define all the expected variations for the decision-making logic and then build table-driven code. Any time a module has been built with table-driven approaches it is worth evaluating it to see if it is automating a decision.

Table-driven code is used to make code easier to change. This is important for automated decisions. Table-driven code does not improve transparency. Often table-driven code is even harder to read as code must be cross-referenced with data tables before it can be understood. In addition, it is often impossible to define all the possible variations so that they can be built into the tables. Code changes will still be required, even if many changes can be made simply by updating tables. If the table-driven code implements a decision, add it to your inventory.

Event-centric

For organizations that are adopting event-centric design and building event processing systems, analyzing existing event-based systems can also result in the identification of additional decisions. Event-based systems are generally high performance, low latency systems, so any decision they require is going to be an excellent Digital Decisioning candidate.

Event-based systems involve many decisions about the events and how to handle them. These are largely internal to the systems themselves. Because of the need for high—often extreme—performance, event-based systems often include business decision-making along with event correlation decisions. A good indication that a decision is embedded in an event-processing system is that it must look up stateless data externally. If the decision is not extracted, the event systems will embed the decision-making logic within their event processing logic and execute it once the data has been retrieved.

For example, an event-based system is ideally suited to monitor a package delivery system. In this way various undesirable states can be detected and acted on in the shortest time possible. Specific data on each package in transit is continually available as a data feed. As the data passes through the event processing system the system builds up a memory of what occurs—both for the individual package itself and systemically for the entire system. The event-based system can correlate data across every package and it can determine that the time difference between packages arriving and leaving a particular hub is increasing exponentially. This could be caused by snowstorms that have closed the airport with a few trucks being used to route the packages out to another hub. The system now needs to prioritize which packages will be moved first on to trucks so they can proceed without any further delay.

The information needed to prioritize packages does not exist within the event-based system. For instance, the company may choose to prioritize by customer membership levels, to ensure that its best customers are given top service. A Gold level member's package might be retrieved from a stranded airplane and loaded on a truck ahead of a package heading to a customer with basic level membership. Information on customer membership levels is typically held in a separate customer database. The event-based package monitoring systems now calls out to this database using the customer information on each stranded package. The ones returned as Gold level customers have their packages rerouted first.

In fact, there is a separate decision here—a decision to determine which customers should be prioritized. This should not be embedded in the event processing system. Instead the decision should be externalized. The clue to the decision was the external look up for additional stateless data.

Documenting Decisions

Before deciding which decisions should be the basis for Digital Decisioning, it is important to understand those decisions. Like any other requirement or specification, decisions can be described in many ways to help clarify how they can be automated. Decisions can also be decomposed so that the way in which a decision is made can be seen more clearly. Understanding the dependencies of a decision on other decisions and on Input Data and Knowledge Sources helps ensure that artificial intelligence technology will be applied correctly. This decomposition of a decision into smaller, more focused decisions can also help balance human and automated decision making. Decisions are also a part of a broader business design, and the linkages between decisions and business processes, events and more help establish its context.

> **Decision Model and Notation**
>
> The Decision Model and Notation (DMN) standard was first published in 2014 and represent an industry-standard way of documenting decisions. The rest of this chapter follows the DMN standard. For a more detailed description of how to model decisions, refer to Taylor and Purchase, 2017.

Decision Basics: Question and Answer

As with most requirements, decisions can be given a name and described. Identifying the "Approve Claim" decision and describing the basic decision-making approach for approving a claim is a good place to start with documenting this decision. Because decisions select from known and defined alternatives, the most powerful information to add to this is a question and a set of possible answers. Extending our example, you could add, "Should this claim be approved for full payment at this time?" as a question and identify, "Yes" and "No" as possible answers.

The question that goes with a decision needs to be as precise as possible. It is helpful to be specific about the subject of the question—the claim in our example—and about the question itself. Identifying a singular subject is also important. If we are approving a specific claim rather than deciding if a group of claims is approved, we should be clear in the question. Time periods and the possibility of re-assessment can also be included in the question. In our example question, we make it clear that claims approval can be decided at multiple times. Questions, like names and descriptions, can also evolve as our understanding improves and clarity is important enough that changes should be allowed.

The set of answers should be complete. The example is a simple one—only Yes and No are allowed. In most questions, the answers are more complex and more varied. The list of allowed answers can be defined explicitly with every possible answer listed, or it can be defined implicitly by reference to some set. A list of allowed answers, for instance, might be "a valid product in the product catalog." When implicit definitions are used, they too should be precise—not "a product" but "a valid product in the product catalog".

Various forms of answers are possible:

1. A number or date from within a range
   E.g. the discount rate to be offered to a customer or the price for a product configuration

2. A single answer value from a set
   E.g. Yes or a product from the product catalog

3. A block of text
   E.g. a customized letter or script

4. A combination consisting of multiple answer values and numbers (the combination is considered a single answer)
   E.g. a product from the product catalog and a specific price for that product

5. Multiple candidate answers from a set each
   E.g. the most suitable 3 products from the catalog with a price for each. Each answer is of the first three kinds of answer—a number, an answer value or a combination of numbers and values.

Spend time getting the allowed answers right

It is worth spending a fair amount of time getting the allowed answers right for a decision. A clear understanding of the available answers will make it much easier to define and manage the decision going forward. The answers show how broad and how complex the decision will need to be. The answers are also how one decision supports another. A clear understanding of the answers will allow the dependencies between decisions to be evaluated.

Many decisions involve both coming up with answers and supporting those answers with explanations or supporting facts. A decision to grant credit may result in a number for the amount of credit granted along with five explanatory statements that explain why the amount was neither higher nor lower. While this information is not part of the answer, it should also be documented as part of the decision.

Linking to the Business

Decisions are independent objects that will repay an investment in being managed independently of other requirements, business processes, events, and systems. They are also essential to these other requirements and it is vital that it is understood how decisions support other elements of the business. The initial discovery of decisions will provide some links to the business. Decisions found in the context of a process are clearly linked to that process. Decisions found in legacy systems analysis are linked to the system in which they were found. Decisions are often reused, so additional links between processes, systems, events, and decisions should be expected and documented when found.

Establishing some other links will make it easier to manage the decisions and easier to determine how best to measure them and improve them over time. Decisions can be linked to the organizational units—departments, people, teams, roles—that are responsible for them. This responsibility might be one of ownership—being responsible for the definition of exactly how the decision should be made—or one of execution—making the individual decision. These are often not the same for repeatable decisions. For instance, a marketing team might own the definition of a cross-sell offer decision, while the call center team owns the execution of that decision.

Measurement of decisions is critical. All decisions have an impact on the metrics and measures that judge success or failure in an organization. If an organization has any control over a metric or an objective, then it must be making decisions that influence that metric. Understanding which decisions impact which metrics, as well as how and why is an essential ingredient in measuring decisions. More importantly, the linkage of decisions to metrics and key performance indicators underpins continuous improvement. Changes to decision making or experiments in decision-making approaches need to be assessed to see which ones should be kept and which rejected. Without a link to the organization's metrics, such assessment will remain technical in nature where it should be business focused.

Modeling Requirements

The day-to-day operations of any organization rely on a portfolio of repeatable decisions. These decisions have a measurable impact on the organization and clearly support its business processes and events. However, the repeatable decisions that support a business are not generally independent of each other. A decision is dependent on another decision if it cannot be made without knowing the outcome of the other decision. Decisions are also dependent on information if they cannot be made without that information, and similarly, on knowledge. Understanding these dependencies links the otherwise isolated decisions discovered into a true portfolio and identifies sub-decisions to give structure to the internal workings of decisions. These dependencies are known as requirements and can be modeled using DMN.

The process for finding decision requirements involves five steps:

1. Determine requirements
2. Find decision requirements
3. Find Input Data
4. Find Knowledge Sources
5. Iterate

The end-result of this analysis is a set of decision requirements diagrams such as that shown in Figure 5-2 that together make up a decision requirements model. This example follows the DMN notation and Decisions are shown as rectangles with Input Data as ovals and Knowledge Sources as documents.

In this model, the decision is whether or not to *Approve Claim*. Making this decision requires information about a *Claim* (shown as an Input Data) and knowledge of i (shown as a Knowledge Source). In addition, it is necessary to first make five other decisions:

- Is the information complete (*Additional Claim Information Needed* decision)
- Is the claimant eligible to make a claim (*Claimant Eligibility* decision)
- Is the claim legal and appropriate (*Appropriateness of Claim* decision)
- Can someone else be held liable for paying the claim (i decision)
- And is there excessive risk of fraud (idecision)

Each of these decisions in turn requires Input Data and applies Knowledge Sources as appropriate. In reality, each of these decisions would also likely depend on further sub-decisions.

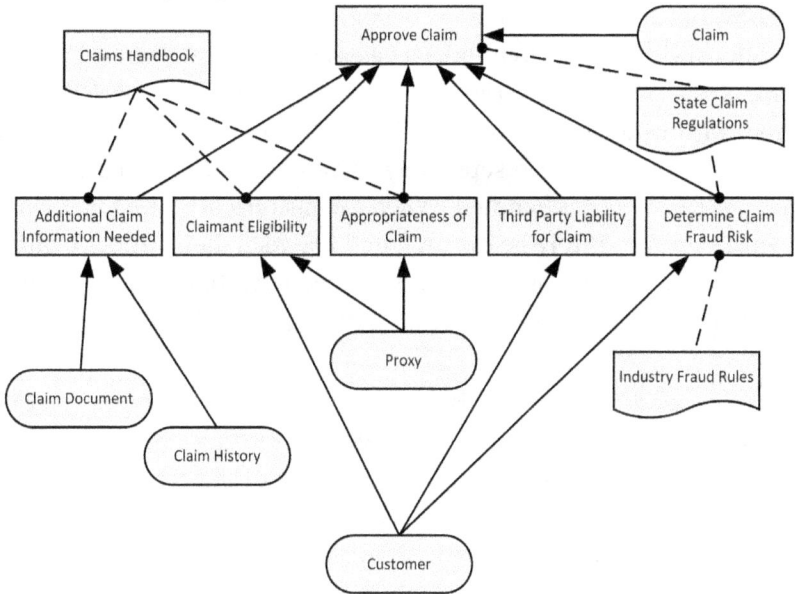

Figure 5-2 *A decision requirements diagram*

Determine Requirements

The most effective way to determine the dependencies of a decision is to work with a group of people who understand how that decision is made today or should be made going forward. Such a group can be asked to list everything needed to make that decision. Each element required for the decision can be listed out. The list will contain elements that are the outcomes of other decisions, elements that are information about the transaction or customer concerned, and elements that are knowledge-related. Each element can be classified and then expanded on depending on its classification.

In the absence of a suitable group of experts, it may be possible to determine the dependencies from existing processes and system implementations but working with the experts is very strongly preferred.

Find Decision Requirements

The most common kind of requirement is a dependency on another decision. Most decisions have dependencies on other pre-cursor decisions or on more granular "sub-decisions." For example, the decision to validate a claim can be decomposed into a decision to confirm the claimant, another to establish completeness of data and a third to validate that individual data elements such as address are valid. It is entirely possible that these decisions have already been identified as part of our decision inventory. For instance, the *Claimant Eligibility* decision might have been separately identified as part of defining how a request for service is handled. When a decision exists already, then the dependency can simply be documented between them. More common is that these other decisions have not yet been identified. In this case, the basic question and answers for each new decision identified need to be documented.

The dependencies in decision requirement models can get quite complex. As the model grows, evaluate the outcomes of all dependent decisions to see if they are enough to support the parent decision. As your understanding of each decision improves, it may become increasingly obvious that there is missing information that implies another dependent decision.

Don't create dependency loops

One challenge with dependency networks, especially deep ones, is that loops can be created where decision A depends on decision B which depends on decision C that in turn depends on decision A. Such loops cannot be valid, and decision requirements models should be checked regularly to ensure such loops are not being created.

As dependent decisions are identified, it will be clear that some of them can be described explicitly using business rules or decision logic while others are more probabilistic or analytical. There may be decisions that will need to be expressed as complex mathematical formulas and others that must find optimal or viable solutions from a wide set of options. As decisions are modeled, identify those that can be represented explicitly using business logic. Try also to identify those that will require particular analytic, optimization or machine learning techniques. The kind of Input Data, the amount of Input Data and the types of knowledge you identify for each decision will provide strong indications of which decision type you are dealing with.

The decisions on which a decision is dependent can also be evaluated as a set. Sometimes there are dependencies between those decisions that should be modeled. In a *Validate Claim* example, for instance, we might initially identify *Confirm Claimant* and *Check For Identity Fraud* as two decisions on which the *Validate Claim* decision is dependent. On further analysis, we might decide it makes more sense for the *Confirm Claimant* decision to be dependent on the *Check For Identity Fraud* decision. In these circumstances, we would remove the direct dependency between *Validate Claim* and *Check For Identity Fraud*, as we have an implied dependency through the *Confirm Claimant* decision.

Find Input Data

Decisions are often dependent on other decisions. In addition, they are often dependent on Input Data. Business decisions cannot be made without some information being presented for consideration. This data might be of various types and can be internal or external to an organization. Information might be about customers, transactions, or the organization itself. All such information should be identified as Input Data and linked to make it clear which Input Data is essential for which decisions.

Avoid detailed data design

It is not useful to try and drive a detailed data design at this stage so business-level Input Data such as "customer profile" or "claim data" are entirely appropriate. If Input Data must be heavily analyzed before it can be used, this is a sign that knowledge (see below) is required—that the decision is actually dependent on the insight derived and not on the base information. For instance, a credit decision is dependent on the likelihood of default which is derived through the analysis of past payment history. The likelihood of default is also a decision, made by applying the knowledge derived from this analysis to the base information.

The organization that is responsible for the data can be recorded and, if known, the data structure noted. Input Data can also be described in terms of the kind of data involved (structured data, structured content and unstructured content).

Structured data is stored in a database, typically a relational one, and the structure of the data—its attributes and allowed values—is known or at least knowable. Every record or instance matches the defined structure, and the data can be manipulated record by record, attribute by attribute, typically very efficiently and rapidly.

Structured content is document- or file-based and typically stored in a content management system. This content also has a repeatable structure that is defined—a contract, for example, has a repeatable structure with parties, clauses and sub-clauses, etc. XML documents or documents with standard contents can be considered structured content.

Unstructured content has no pre-defined structure, such as call notes or the body of an email. Analysis of this information and its use in Digital Decisioning is more complex than the use of structured data and content, but it is increasingly common. Analysis includes entity extraction, text analysis, sentiment analysis, and assessing how likely it is that the text is discussing a particular topic.

Managing external data costs with Digital Decisioning

There is a whole class of Digital Decisioning focused on decisions about external data. Some external data sources can improve a decision but cost a significant amount per transaction. It can be very valuable to determine if the external data will actually make any difference before paying for it. Digital Decisioning may be used to make this determination. For instance, in auto insurance, it costs a significant amount to request a Motor Vehicle Report on a driver to confirm their driving record. Digital Decisioning may be applied to determine if the information in such a report will make any difference to the underwriting process or even if it will make a difference larger than the cost of the report. This will eliminate unnecessary costs.

Find Knowledge

Decisions also rely on knowledge. As you decompose decisions, identify the Knowledge Sources those decisions rely on. Knowledge Sources fall into four broad categories—Policies, Regulations, Analytic insight and Expertise. For instance, a decision on the eligibility of a person to claim a government benefit is dependent on the regulations that define the criteria for that eligibility.

Policies and regulations are available in documents and publications. Regulations might be produced by local, state, or national governments. Policies may be internal to the organization, passed on to it by a parent or related organization, or published by an industry group. These documents may define limitations on how specific decisions can be made and provide guidance on how to make a good decision. The documents are unlikely to only contain decision-related material. More typically, policies and regulations contain requirements for processes as well as more general guidance for organizations. Policy and regulation know-how should be defined at a level that makes sense. For instance, an organization might differentiate between the regulations from the Federal government and those from State governments, while not listing every individual state regulation as a separate source.

Capturing the data needs for analytic insight

When you identify analytic insight as being necessary for making a decision it is important to think through the data that this analytic insight will require. This information may be modeled as Input Data already, but it may not be. For instance, a decision on customer retention may require analytic insight about the risk of a customer canceling their service. This insight may require analysis of their social network—their friends and family members—to see if anyone in the network has left recently. This information is not Input Data used directly by any of the decisions being modeled. Document this kind of information as part of the analytic insight as you refine your understanding of how you will derive the insight you need.

Analytic insight is knowledge derived from data analysis. It could be developed using business intelligence, data mining, predictive analytics, machine learning, text analytics or some combination of approaches. When the *insight* gained from information matters to how a decision is made, then a link to an analytic Knowledge Source is required. Often a sub-decision must also be added to make the analytic decision. For instance, a decision to decide the likelihood that a claimant has an undisclosed medical condition. This is based on analytic insight derived from past cases and should be linked both to the Input Data representing those cases and to the Knowledge Source representing the results of the analysis.

The final category is that of expertise. Many decisions are dependent on the accumulated experience and wisdom of those who have been making the decision for a while. This might be called collective wisdom or tribal knowledge. Decisions are typically dependent on this kind of know-how because it helps make good decisions. Often the best way, at least while data is being gathered and analyzed, to tell how to make a good decision is to use the experience and judgment of those who have been making effective decisions. For example, the best practices of the procurement department might be the best source of knowledge for selecting suppliers, and decisions in this area would then be dependent on this Knowledge Source.

Determine if Multiple Approaches Are Required

When a decision is driven entirely by regulation or policy, there will generally only be a single decision-making approach to be implemented. All transactions will be handled using the same decision-making approach. Only the approach defined by the policies and regulations is permissible. For instance, a decision to determine if a citizen is eligible for a particular benefit will have a single path for all citizens with the same values in the input information. If it involves judgment or expertise, rules derived from data, predictive analytic models or machine learning algorithms, then alternative approaches will be worth considering for the decision.

When multiple approaches are possible, it is often not possible to tell which approach results in the right or "best" answer for some time. When we reach the point of being able to assess how effective our decision making was, it will be useful if we can compare several different approaches to see which worked best. In the absence of a time machine, we cannot go back and re-test a new approach on the same customers. We must therefore experiment, treating two similar customers differently so we can see which approach will work best.

Making decisions using multiple similar approaches allows different applications of judgment and different analytic approaches to be compared in terms of their impact on actual transactions or customers.

> **Take your time analyzing decision-making approaches**
>
> Alterative decision-making approaches in a Decision Service allow you to compare their effect on real transactions as they flow through your processes and systems. This is often the only way to really tell which approach works better or what the differences are in terms of outcomes. Design-time comparisons as well as simulation should also be used to compare decision-making approaches. An approach should not be considered for use in a deployed Decision Service unless analysis using historical data implies that it might work well.

If the current decision-making approach has no particular significance and there is no reason to believe that one approach will be better than another going forward, then an A/B testing approach can be applied. In this approach, several equally good approaches can be considered with the transactions distributed evenly between them. Marketing and other opportunity decisions often fall in this category. There are few restrictions on how the decision can be made and no particular reason to believe that one approach is better than others. While A/B testing implies two approaches, some decisions conduct this kind of testing of equally valid approaches for 3 or more approaches - A/B/C testing, if you will.

The decision-making approaches implemented will generally all be variations on a theme. They may make one or more different assumptions about what will work or what a customer will find compelling. They might vary the messaging for an offer or the offer itself or apply different pricing and discount approaches. The resulting decisions are similar, but by running multiple approaches in parallel, you will be able to tell which is more effective in terms of its impact on business results.

When the current approach cannot lightly be changed or when there is a clear case that one approach will probably be best, A/B testing will be inappropriate. When the current approach has a long and successful history or when there are clear best practices for a decision-making approach, there will be strong pressure to use this approach for all decisions. After all it is likely to be the best so why wouldn't you want to treat all customers this way? If alternatives to such a strong decision-making approach seem worth considering then you should adopt a champion-challenger approach.

In this case most transactions are run through the established or *champion* approach. This ensures that most customers continue to be treated using the established best practice. A small percentage of all transactions are not handled with this decision making approach. Instead they are processed using one of potentially several *challenger* decision-making approaches. This approach creates data about the effectiveness of these alternatives while minimizing the number of decisions impacted by the alternatives.

Sometimes the challengers have only small differences from the champion, and the purpose of conducting the experiment is to see if a small change can make the current champion a little more effective. Sometimes, however, there is a sense that the current approach has been refined and tuned to a "local maximum." In these circumstances, any small change is going to be worse than the champion, so only more radical alternatives are worth considering. Sometimes a combination is appropriate—several incremental changes are tested as challengers as well as one "out there" approach.

Multiple decision-making approaches

Some decisions don't have an obvious "best" way for the decision to be made. For others, the business may want the ability to run experiments comparing different decision-making approaches. At this stage identifying the decisions that would need to vary, or that could be varied, is likely to be sufficient. The actual implementation of multiple decision-making approaches into the Decision Service can be left until later and is described in the next chapter. Some of this design work can be done at this stage if that seems helpful or if the business experts have already done a significant amount of design thinking about the approaches they need.

Because each challenger only handles a small number of transactions, this approach minimizes the risk of trying something radically different while still gathering the data necessary to see if that radical approach is worth trying.

To add multiple decision-making approaches, identify the decisions that will be made differently in your alternative approaches. Each decision-approach pair will be a decision in the model. Every decision in the model dependent on those decisions will need to be varied – those decisions will be made differently by applying one or other of the alternative approaches to their sub-decisions. Each such decision should be given a sub-decision for each of the alternative approaches. Each of these will make the same decision – answer the same question – in a different way and the original decision will simply pick the relevant answer based on the approach selected. Most of the sub-decisions of these decisions will not vary between approaches and so can be reused – only the decisions central to the alternative approaches will be different.

In the Figure 5-3 below, for instance, three approaches are being compared. One determines what complete documentation would be, one determines the minimum documentation and one a moderate compromise set of documentation. These three decisions reuse other Decisions and Input Data.

Iterate

As the decision requirements model is developed, it will be necessary to repeat this decomposition at each new level. When a decision is decomposed to show the decisions it depends on it is likely that new decisions will be created. These decisions must not only be described, they must also be decomposed in turn. Eventually a set of "atomic" decisions that cannot be usefully broken down any further will be identified. All the dependent decisions will exist. At that point, the decision model can be considered stable. It is likely to change in the future, but decision discovery can move on to understanding and documenting the details of the decisions that have been identified.

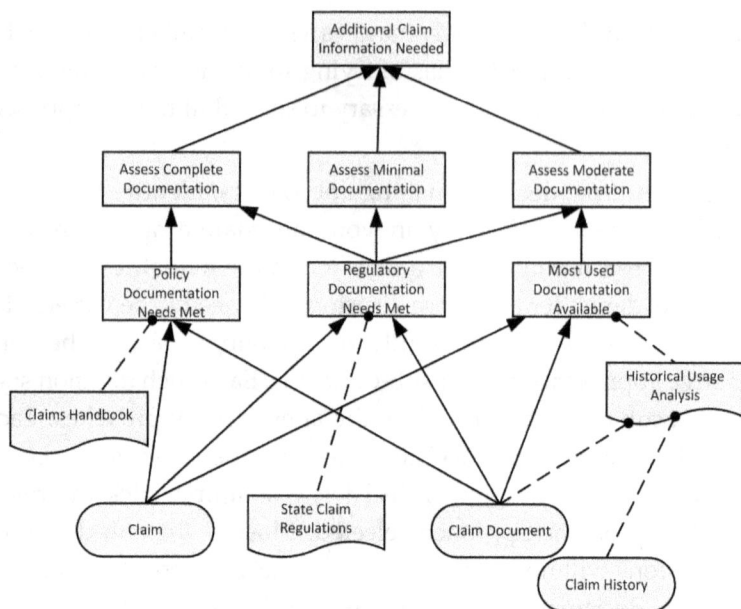

Figure 5-3 Multiple Approaches To Claims Documentation

Document Decision Logic Requirements

Many of the decisions in a decision requirements model can be defined as decision logic. These are going to be implemented using business rules to represent this decision logic. When the end implementation of a decision is expected to involve business rules, it is helpful to capture more details about the decision logic expected beyond just the Knowledge Sources that contain it. Decision logic requirements are captured one decision at a time – each decision in the model has its own decision logic.

There's a lot more to writing business rules

It is not the intent of this book to define a complete approach for finding, documenting, or developing business rules. For instance, we will not be discussing the development of glossaries (a common step in defining business rules) nor the details of appropriate syntax.

Decision logic requirements are documented using various easy to understand approaches focused on natural language descriptions of what should be done when a specific set of conditions are true – business

102

rules. These may be written in an "If this is true then do that" format or as "When this is true do that" but they are most commonly documented using decision tables. A decision table lays out a set of rules – the logic for a complete decision – in a tabular format. The columns represent the information used to make the decision – the information requirements – and each row represents a rule. Each row documents the combination of values in the information requirements that results in a specific action. This determines which of the allowed actions for that decision should be selected when the various information requirements have those values. Compact and clear, decision tables are a very effective tool for documenting decision logic and reviewing it with business owners.

The table in Figure 5-4, for instance, shows seven rules in a tabular layout that each consider the asset category of an asset, its issuer class and whether or not it is convertible to determine its asset class.

Issuer Based Asset Class				
U	Asset Category	Instrument is Convertible	Issuer Class	Issuer Based Asset Class
1	OTHER	-	-	OTHER
2	INDEX	-	-	INDEX
3	EQUITY	-	-	EQUITY
4	PREFERRED	true	-	CVTPFD
5		false	-	OTHER
6	DEBT	true	-	CONVERTIBLE
7	DEBT	false	SUPRA	SUPRA

Figure 5-4 Simple Asset Class Decision Table

When documenting decision logic requirements, the most important thing is clarity to 'those who run the business. No restriction should be placed on how rules are documented at this stage as restrictions of this type can reduce the clarity for the business people involved in the project. This does not mean that you cannot define a style for these rules or insist on using defined terms and vocabulary. You should just ensure that these restrictions improve business clarity and are supported and understood by the non-technical business experts critical to effectively identifying your decision logic requirements.

Business rules or decision logic may be represented in some or all of the Knowledge Sources in the decision requirements network. When legacy systems are being reengineered rules can be found in legacy code.

They are also found as additional types of knowledge—policies and regulations, expertise, or tribal knowledge and data analysis.

Never just harvest business rules

Many organizations set out to harvest all the business rules in their existing systems as a precursor to digital decisioning. This is never worthwhile, resulting in a "big bucket of rules" that is of little or no use.

Digital decisioning relies on developing robust, accurate descriptions of the decision logic needed. Capturing decision logic, business rules, only in the context of a decision model is critical.

Always begin with a decision model. Only extract or document business rules or decision logic in this context. The decision model groups related rules together as part of how a single sub-decision is made. A decision model keeps business rules consistent, laying out the data available to the rules using the information requirements. It clarifies the purpose of the rules through the allowed answers of the decision. Without this structure only very poor quality business rules can be captured.

In Legacy Systems

Various tools exist for extracting business rules from legacy code. Even though these tools can provide useful input to defining the business rules or decision logic of a decision, it is generally not helpful to use the extracted rules going forward. The extracted rules tend to be too technical for business users to review or edit and too linked to the legacy implementation to make good rules in the new environment.

Legacy systems can provide data insight

Legacy systems can also provide useful information on the data that has historically been used in the decision as well as the set of allowed actions for a decision.

Instead, the intended and observed behavior of the legacy system can be used to define the decisions and decision logic implied by the legacy system. These decisions can be validated against the extracted rules. Real differences of behavior are likely for one of two reasons. The legacy system may have problems. If it does, these are likely to be known. The legacy system may contain fixes that are not known to those outside of IT. It is not uncommon, for instance, for regulations to have inconsistencies. A legacy system might have additional rules encoded to deal with these inconsistencies. Capturing these additional business rules so that the decision model can handle those same inconsistencies is important.

Sometimes staff turnover or situational complexity means that the only way to see what the legacy system does is to analyze the code and extract rules. In these circumstances, begin with the extracted "technical" rules. Then manually derive more business-oriented rules from them by replacing technical terms with their business equivalent. And also by generalizing specific processing behavior into the business behavior it represents. As always, make sure these business rules are specific to decisions in your decision model.

Legacy systems are a poor source of business rules

In general, legacy systems are a poor choice for decision logic identification and should be used only when there is no alternative. However, analyzing existing code to see what "technical" rules are implied by that code *is* an effective check on business rules developed directly from policies or regulations.

In Policies and Regulations

The most productive way to derive rules in many circumstances is to begin with the policies or regulations that must be enforced in the decision. Regulations come from outside the organization while policies come from inside. They can be treated in very similar ways when it comes to extracting decision logic. Both policies and regulations contain things that must be enforced as well as suggestions or advice. Both also contain information about how to execute processes, handle data, or perform other non-decision-making tasks.

Extracting rules from policies and regulations is mostly an exercise in identifying those statements that say how a decision should, must, or could be made from the other statements in the document. Often done as part of a broader analysis of a policy or regulation, this extraction process results in a set or perhaps several sets of rules.

Each policy or regulation is modeled as a Knowledge Source and the decisions that require that Knowledge Source are those for which rules must be written based on the policy or regulation. As a policy or regulation is analyzed it may be that rules are found that seem unrelated to these decisions, probably because the regulation applies also to other decisions that have not yet been modeled. Rules extracted from policies or regulations should be captured in the decisions to which they relate.

From Experts

As with many information systems projects, interviewing experts is almost certain to be important when seeking business rules. Typical knowledge elicitation techniques can be applied to help experts tell you what rules they follow when making a specific decision in the model. Most will be able to document many rules and guidelines quickly, at least for the core or most common transaction types.

Identify Critical Agility Needs

When documenting decision logic, keep track of decisions where agility is likely to be critical. It is often obvious from the initial analysis that the rules for a decision or set of sub-decisions will change regularly. The need for particularly rapid changes, in response to lawsuits for instance, is also generally easy to identify. Make sure these decisions and their decision logic are designed with business agility in mind.

Getting decision logic requirements for the less common or corner cases and so ensuring that all the rules have been gathered is a different issue. Especially for more complex decisions, experts will not be able to define all their rules in a top-down fashion. Instead, use actual cases to help elicit the remaining rules. Apply the core rules extracted to a corner case and show the resulting decision to the expert. If there are additional rules that are relevant to that corner case, the expert will be able to reject the proposed decision and explain why they did so. This explanation will identify the remaining rules for that case. Repeated over several corner cases, this will result in a more complete set of rules.

> **Don't wait to capture all the rules**
>
> It is not necessary to capture all the business rules before beginning. One of the most important features of Digital Decisioning is the ability to evolve and improve decision-making over time. As long as there is a safe default response that can be offered when you cannot make a decision, it is easy to gradually enhance your decision-making to handle more cases. For instance, initial versions may not handle any of the corner cases where applicants provide supporting information, referring all those applicants to a manual process. Over time the various corner cases may be investigated and additional business rules added to handling these cases.

From Data

One of the most neglected sources of business rules is the historical data that an organization has collected about what was done in the past. This contains the results of applying the rules in place at the time, as well as representing a record that can be mined for what works and what does not.

There are several data mining and machine learning techniques that automatically create business rules explicitly or in the form of decision trees. The techniques are broadly similar in terms of the output they generate—the key difference between the various methods is the way in which they create the business rules or decision trees.

Some data mining algorithms are more amenable than others in being able to be represented as business rules. Decision Tree-based algorithms, such as CART, CHAID, and C5, are also known as Rule Induction models because they generate a model suitable for representation as a set of rules. Each algorithm will use slightly different methods to build the tree (or the rules) and will have different options that affect how the tree is grown. In each case the end result is the same—a predictive analytic model that can be represented as a series of If…Then rules that select segments of cases that you wish to target or exclude.

> **Data mining produces executable business rules**
>
> The rules produced by data mining and machine learning algorithms are typically executable business rules. It may be helpful to regard the output of the data mining or the model itself as the implementation of the decision. Often this involves a 1:1 mapping—the execution is the same as the original model output. Sometimes there are differences because some interpretation is involved. Treating the original data mining results as decision logic requirements rather than an executable decision will then be helpful.

Association rule algorithms such as Apriori and Carma are also good candidates for generating rule-based predictions. These algorithms are often used to find the items that occur together in a transactional set of data, such as items in a shopping basket. They can also be used to identify events that occur together in a sequence, useful for identifying patterns in time-based processes. Depending on the situation, these algorithms can help to identify the most common patterns or find the rare outliers that may indicate that something has occurred that shouldn't have. For example, the model might identify the products that most commonly get purchased together to better cross sell related products.

For organizations that have invested in business rules, representing analytic results as business rules is often an effective way to benefit quickly from the output of machine learning in their operational environment. Representing predictive analytic models as business rules is less intimidating for those not familiar with the machine learning techniques or technologies involved. This can increase the acceptance and interpretability of a model and improve the odds that it will be used. Presenting the model in this way can also allow for partial implementation if one part is more controversial than another. It does introduce an additional step and associated delay into the development process.

It is common to see organizations initially define all their decision logic requirements as business rules. They first look at their data simply to validate these business rules. They may then start to apply some simple data mining or machine learning algorithms to their data to suggest new business rules. As they become more confident that their data is a good source of decision logic, they will be more willing to consider simply using a predictive analytic, machine learning or other artificial intelligence algorithm directly. Taking the time to walk an organization along such a path can ease analytic adoption.

Some analytic models should not be represented as business rules

There are several common predictive analytic models that cannot easily be represented and executed as business rules. These include Linear and Logistic Regression Models, Time Series models, and other statistical based algorithms that must be represented as a statistical equation. Those based on Neural Networks and some segmentation models such as K-Means, Two Step, and Kohonen are generally not easy to represent as business rules because their execution relies on statistical equations or on neural networks. Machine learning algorithms of all kinds are often hard to represent as business rules. In these circumstances, the predictive analytic model is the whole decision. Do not force fit any analytic model to a set of business rules unless there is value in doing so.

6. Build Decision Services

An organization that has discovered and modeled a decision or a set of decisions is ready to begin automation. The characteristics and decomposition of those decisions provide a detailed specification of the decision, how it is made, its actions and more. This specification is used to build Decision Services.

Decision Services are service-oriented components that make decisions. The main step in implementing Digital Decisioning is to define and build a Decision Service that delivers the selected decision as an IT component. This Decision Service will also need to be integrated with the rest of the IT environment.

Decision Services require decision scaffolding to handle the flow of the decision as well as the predictive analytic models from machine learning, business rules, and optimization models that determine how the decision should be made. For many decisions, a test and learn infrastructure will also be required.

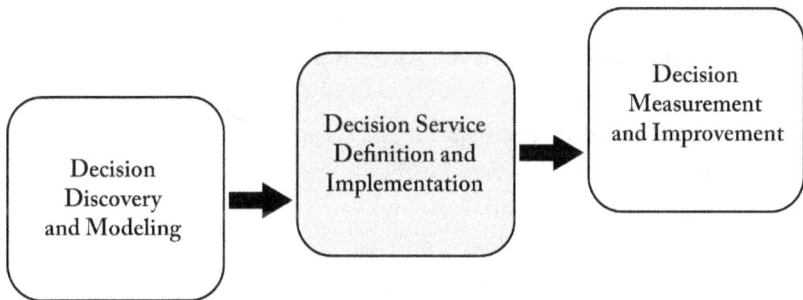

Figure 6-1 Decision Service Definition and Implementation in Context

Define Decision Services

A Decision Service implements one or more of the decisions identified and modeled. A Decision Service answers a set of questions for other systems, processes or services—the questions defined for the decisions it implements.

Decision Services are not implemented for every decision identified in the decision inventory. In general, the highest-level decisions possible should be turned into Decision Services—those decisions that are required by a process or an event, or that replace a module in a legacy application. These high-level decisions are those that offer the most value when built as Decision Services. Lower level decisions are useful for designing these Decision Services but may not be worth deploying as a Decision Service in their own right. A Decision Service should only be built for these lower-level decisions if there are processes, events, or systems that need access to these sub-decisions other than in the context of the top-level decisions. Often, a single Decision Service can have multiple entry points to allow access to these lower-level decisions. The ability to reuse business rules, analytic models, and optimization components between Decision Services based on a common decision model means that there is no need to incur the overhead of a Decision Service to access these sub-decisions.

Building a Decision Service involves laying out the decision itself including any support for multiple decision-making approaches, building the scaffolding for the decision-making components, and then developing the analytic models, business rules, and optimization models necessary to make the decision. By far the best way to develop Decision Services is iteratively, gradually improving the quality of decisions or the percentage of decisions handled over time.

Build Decision Scaffolding

The core elements of the Decision Service are implemented as business rules, predictive analytic models (including those built using machine learning approaches), and optimization models. To ensure these elements are used together in an appropriate way, a Decision Service requires some scaffolding. This scaffolding brings the right decision-making components together in the right order to produce the intended result.

The first step is to define a Decision Service against the decision model. DMN contains a Decision Service concept designed to be overlain on a decision requirements model. Identify the decisions that the Decision Service needs to be able to make – the output or invokable decisions. Next, define the decision that will be encapsulated in the Decision Service. This may be all the decisions required directly or indirectly by the invokable decisions or it may be a subset of those decisions. The Decision Service will need to be able to execute all the encapsulated decisions and respond to requests for any or all of the invokable decisions.

The decision model and associated Decision Service design contains much useful information that can be used to derive the necessary decision scaffolding. It contains a definition of the allowed actions for the decisions that can be invoked and a model of the various sub-decisions, Input Data, and Knowledge Sources that the decision is dependent on. In addition, the context(s) in which the Decision Service is accessed are defined in terms of the business processes, events, and systems that will use the decision being implemented.

The Decision Service definition defines a service contract for the Decision Service. Such a contract states that given a certain set of information, the Decision Service will answer a particular question and commit to returning one of the allowed answers along with any supporting information. It defines the outputs produced and inputs required by the Decision Service.

- **Outputs**: An examination of the question and allowed answers defines part of the service contract. The allowed answers show what can be returned by the Decision Service in business terms. These are used to derive a more formal definition of the output from the Decision Service. For instance, a claims processing decision might have allowed answers of "Fast Track," "Refer" and "Investigate." As part of defining the service contract, we might decide to return a string containing one of these three allowed values or a number with each value representing a particular answer.

  Many decisions return supporting information in addition to the formal answer. This supporting information should be analyzed similarly to formally define the additional information that may be returned. For instance, if the claims processing decision also involves returning some reasons for the action recommended along with associated reason codes (a common set of additional information), we will define an array of reason codes—reason text pairs as an additional part of the contract.

  Decision Services should also write a log of the decision-making that executed but this is generally written out separately to a data lake or data warehouse rather than being returned as an output.

- **Inputs**: While our model of a decision gave us a very specific set of outputs, we have only a high-level definition of the inputs required by the decision. Examining the dependency network to see all the Input Data on which the decision is dependent, or on which its dependent decisions are themselves dependent, will give us a starting point. This can be formally defined by overlaying a Decision Service on the decision model and seeing which information requirements cross the Decision Service boundary.

  In addition, a review of the contexts in which the decision is required will show what information is likely to be available at that point in the process or system or when the event occurs. Based on the analysis of these inputs, a contract can also be defined for the Input Data.

Don't over constrain Input Data

While it is a good idea to define a contract for the Decision Service first, the data used by a decision may evolve as the Decision Service is constructed. It may become apparent as business rules are written or machine learning models integrated that additional data must be available beyond what was originally expected.

To reduce the need to change the contract, it is better to specify all the Input Data available within reason so the contract will not need to change as new requirements are identified within the Decision Service. For instance, if customer data is required by the decision, then include all the customer data typically available in the Input Data, even if there is not yet a defined need for the data within the decision.

For instance, a Decision Service implementing a decision to make a cross-sell offer to a customer as they check out would have a simple output data contract. It needs to return enough information to identify the offer being suggested. Its inputs would be the standard set of information about a customer as well as the contents of the customer's current shopping basket and their order history.

Once the contract is defined, it is possible to do several things. First, a stub can be developed that acts like the Decision Service. This takes the defined inputs and returns the default answer. In our next best offer example, this might be a basic offer available to everyone. This won't be a great offer for anyone but won't be terrible either. A Decision Service that returns this answer every time may not be very useful, but it can be integrated with other services and components. Once such a stub exists, other components can be built or amended to use the Decision Service.

In addition, it is possible to start defining test cases. Knowing the test cases in advance, or at least creating the core set of test cases, makes it much easier to tell when a Decision Service has reached the minimum level for deployment. This is important as Decision Services are rarely as complete or accurate when first deployed as they will become over time. The first version deployed need not be complete or fully refined, but it must meet a basic level of completeness. Defining an initial set of test cases and a test strategy based on the decision description and the contract definition will allow the development of a "version 1" Decision Service that can be safely deployed to start adding value.

Not all Decision Services can be deployed incrementally

Some Decision Services are replacing existing components. In these cases it may not be possible to deploy the Decision Service until it at least meets the level of the component it is replacing. The test cases should reflect that.

Turn the Dependency Network into a Flow

Once the contract of the Decision Service is defined and a set of test cases established, the next step is to define the decision flow. While some decisions contain a single step, most do not. For every Decision Service that requires only the execution of a single optimization model or a single decision table, there are many that involve multiple steps that must be executed against a common set of information in order to determine the right answer to the question.

A decision flow consists of a series of decision making tasks linked together with conditional branches if necessary. A decision flow can be thought of as a kind of decision process. Unlike a true business process,

115

it should not have the ability to assign work to people nor should it include tasks that might take extended periods to execute. Instead, the decision flow should be a set of tightly linked tasks that execute rapidly based on a common set of data to return an answer such that the calling system or process can reliably wait for an answer from the Decision Service.

In the decision discovery phase, we established a dependency network for the top level decision being implemented in the Decision Service. This dependency network can now be used to drive the initial decision flow design. Those sub-decisions on which the decision is dependent make up the tasks in the flow. These sub-decisions may simply go earlier in the flow or may be more appropriately represented by a sub-flow with additional tasks.

Decisions are often dependent on multiple precursor sub-decisions with no particular reason for one of those sub-decisions to be made before another. As the decision flow is a design element, it is now time to make choices about which should go first, second, and so on. For instance, one of the sub decisions on which the main decision is dependent may cause transactions to be rejected. Putting such a task early in the flow would allow rapid rejection of transactions that would be rejected eventually. Tasks may also be defined to execute in parallel.

As the decision flow is laid out, identify which tasks are going to be represented by business rules, which by predictive analytic models developed using machine learning, or optimization models. Orchestrating the various technologies involved to ensure the whole decision is an important role for the decision flow.

The data available throughout the decision flow should also be defined. The primary data involved in the flow is going to be based on the contract defined earlier. The Input Data will be available from the start of the flow, and the output data structure will need to be available so that it can be populated by the various tasks making the decision. Additional information is also produced by the tasks—this information represents the answers produced by the sub-decisions being implemented. Sometimes this data is also part of the output, but sometimes it must be added to the data flowing through the decision. It should always be logged for audit and later analysis so that you can see how you made the decision each time you made it.

Build Test and Learn Infrastructure

As noted above, some decisions benefit from multiple approaches
and experimentation. Either several approaches will be considered as
peers – A/B testing – or a champion approach will be used for most
transactions and compared to several challenger approaches used for a
small minority. When experimentation is necessary, a test-and-learn
infrastructure will need to be built into the Decision Service scaffolding.

To build in test-and-learn infrastructure, examine the decision flow
and identify the sections of that flow where multiple possible
approaches could be considered. This might be the whole flow but
might also be just part of it. In a decision there might be several sections
where a single approach makes sense and several where an ability to try
several approaches will be useful. For each section, the beginning and
end are defined and the enclosed tasks identified. For instance, our
claims decision might include some validation and eligibility tasks
initially that will always be the same for all claims. Once a claim is
determined to be eligible, we may have some tasks to make an
assessment of the likelihood of fraud. In this latter section we might
want to create an ability to try several different approaches to detecting
fraud. This will allow us to compare approaches to see how much fraud
they catch and how many false positives they generate.

For both A/B and Champion/Challenger testing, you create a branch
in the decision flow that will route transactions through one of the
available approaches based on a random assignment. A further branch
then brings all the approaches together again to continue with any
additional tasks.

> **Keep track of the approach used**
>
> You will need to keep track of the decision-making approach used for each transaction. This can be recorded as part of logging the Decision Service behavior, or it can be passed out of the Decision Service as part of the data associated with the answer. If the latter, then it should be part of your service contract. If possible, run all the decision-making approaches for all transactions and store the results for future analysis. Even if you did not act on some of the approaches, knowing what you would have done differently can be very helpful in analysis.

At this point, you have a decision flow outlined that shows how various tasks are executed to take a set of defined Input Data and generate an allowed response, along with any defined supporting data. This now needs to be fleshed out with business rules and predictive analytic models and optimization models.

Implement Decision Services

Determine Objects

Decision logic requirements do not generally refer to the actual objects that exist in the systems with which a Decision Service will be integrated. Business rules and production models/algorithms, on the other hand, must execute against these objects—they must be able to manipulate the objects that exist in the rest of your information systems.

To make this work, you link the objects in your systems—the objects that are being passed to your Decision Service as part of its contract—to the terms and vocabulary that make sense to those who will be writing and reviewing the business rules. Each object and each attribute for each object has a technical definition that allows it to be accessed. The mapping gives each object and each attribute a description useful to someone familiar with the business but not the underlying technology. This mapped vocabulary will replace technical IT terminology with something that matches the way the business team thinks about the things being manipulated with business rules.

The process of creating predictive analytic models using machine learning techniques usually requires the creation of a number of new attributes or features. This might range from creating a variable such as Age by taking a customer's date of birth away from today's date to more complex attributes such as "Number of times in the last 180 days that the customer's payment has been more than 30 days late." These new attributes will need to be added to the objects available to the Decision Service.

> **Consider a feature farm**
>
> If you are using machine learning models extensively or aggressively, the number of features being considered by the machine learning engine can get large. Ensuring that all these features will be available to the Decision Services that use the machine learning models requires real-time access to a "feature farm" that calculates all these features for all transactions as they stream in.

Build Predictive Analytic Models

While many of the decisions in a decision flow will be represented by decision tables or rule sets, some will be represented by predictive analytic models. These mathematical models take a set of information about a customer, a transaction, or some other object and use that information to calculate a score or propensity. The intent of the model is that this score is a probability that something is true. For instance, a predictive analytic model might use information about a claim to predict the likelihood that it is fraudulent. Such a prediction is not absolute but it clarifies our uncertainty. We know some claims are fraudulent, but we are uncertain which ones. The predictive analytic model turns this uncertainty into a usable probability—the likelihood that a particular claim is fraudulent.

Using machine learning to build a predictive analytic model requires access to historical data that includes information on what you are hoping to predict. For instance, if you wish to predict fraudulent claims, then you will need historical data on claims that were determined to be fraudulent as well as data on claims that were valid. This historical data is used to build the model using a variety of mathematical techniques.

Using machine learning to implement decisions in your model can result in more accurate decisions than capturing business rules from experts. Done correctly, machine learning can use actual results to eliminate mistaken beliefs. For complex problems it can be significantly quicker to develop a machine learning model from historical data than it would be to gather business rules from experts.

Building predictive analytic models

It is not the intent of this section to describe the complete process for using machine learning to build predictive analytic models or using other probabilistic artificial intelligence algorithms. Existing methodologies and suitable texts that do describe the complete process are listed in the bibliography. CRISP-DM, the CRoss Industry Standard Process for Data Mining- is the most well established approach and is strongly recommended.

The core steps for building a predictive analytic model are exploring and understanding data that might be predictive, preparing this data, applying various mathematical analysis techniques, building and testing the model, and deploying it.

Business Understanding

In CRISP-DM and all other effective methods for developing predictive analytic model and applying machine learning and artificial intelligence algorithms, the first step is to understand the business problem. When projects begin by developing a decision model, as noted above, this step has already been completed. Because the analytics are being developed to answer a question in the context of a known decision model, there is no need to develop additional business understanding at this time.

Explore and Understand Data

Most predictive analytic models are built from multiple data sources. Once a problem has been clearly identified as one requiring a predictive analytic model, it is essential to explore existing data sources to see how those data sources might contribute to an effective predictive analytic model. In this case the business need is clear: an analytical decision must

120

be made based on some analytic insight derived from historical data.

Each potential data source should be examined for format, quality and quantity both of records and of attributes. Basic statistical analyses can be performed to see if attributes have relationships to each other or if there are large numbers of missing values. The normal range of continuous values in a particular attribute or the set of explicit values used should be determined.

Data privacy regulations

New regulations are starting to give consumers more control over their data. If the data you are considering is covered by these regulations, you will have to exclude the data belonging to consumers who have not consented.

Prepare Data

The raw data available in most data sources is not immediately consumable by the tools and techniques that develop predictive analytic models. It must be cleaned and integrated, sampled if there is a great deal of data, split into training and validation sets, and more. In addition, additional attributes are likely to be created from the data that have greater predictive power than the raw attributes contained in the original data source.

Different analysis techniques require data of different cleanliness; the first step in preparing the data is to make sure that the data is clean enough to be used. This might involve simple steps like substituting for missing values, or more complex ones such as estimating missing data using modeling techniques.

The data from various data sources needs to be integrated so that a combined dataset can be presented to the modeling techniques that will be used to build the predictive model. Typically this involves flattening data that is hierarchical. For instance, when merging a customer data set with an accounts data set, it is likely that some customers have multiple accounts. Flattening this data set would take the important information about accounts and repeat it one, two, three, or more times so that each account would be stored in its own set of attributes. This kind of denormalization is important for most machine learning workbenches and techniques.

One of the most important steps in preparing data is the generation of additional attributes. Most predictive analytic models use a set of attributes only some of which are in the original source data—the rest are calculated. These range from simple calculations such as Age (using today's date and birth date, for instance) to much more complex ones such as Number of times a customer has been more than 30 days late on a payment in the last 180 days. Many such attributes might be created to see if they are potentially predictive and automation of this task is increasingly common.

Finally, it is common and generally recommended to split the data into two sets—one to train the model and one to test it. By excluding all the test data from the model training, we give ourselves a way to test with data that the modeling technique has never "seen." This prevents what is known as "overfitting," where the model is very predictive but only of the data that was used to train it—the model works for the data that built it but not for more general data sets.

Automation in Machine Learning platforms

Modern analytical, machine learning and AI platforms automate many of the steps so that users can build more models more quickly. Such tools often handle training data, sampling, data cleansing, integration and much more. Often the user can simply drag their datasets into a working environment where much of the work of data preparation is completed automatically, needing only to be confirmed. Increasingly this automation is combined with high performance and cloud environments to allow very large volumes of data to be analyzed, avoiding the need to sample.

Select Technique(s)

Many different predictive analytic and machine learning techniques exist. While most are not suitable for some situations and some are particularly good for a type of problem, most predictive analytic models could be developed using one of several techniques. Multiple techniques can also be assembled into what is known as an ensemble model. The growing power of machine learning platforms often allows all the possible techniques to be tried and compared, allowing selection to be based on proven effectiveness.

Build and Test

The various techniques can now be used to build models. Often the same technique can be used to build multiple models with different assumptions or parameters. Once built, all these different models can be compared to see which seems most predictive. The key criterion is the extent to which the model will help improve the decision-making. A model might be more predictive of fraud, for instance, but generate too many false positives and so be rejected in favor of a less predictive model that generates fewer. Machine learning platforms generally automate much of the building and comparison of models so that a user can get the best possible model without having to review each manually.

Models with good potential are validated using the test data held back from the initial modeling effort. Ensembles of multiple models can be constructed and similarly tested. The end result is a preferred or most predictive model.

Deploy

Deploying the model into production so that it can be part of the Decision Service is critical. Without this step, the model will languish on the sidelines, potentially predictive but not being used. Multiple options for deploying the model can be considered, depending on how current the model needs to be and the specifics of the decision being automated.

- Separate machine learning services or APIs can be deployed that are invoked by the Decision Service. These often take advantage of stream architectures to ensure that the calculated attributes required for the analytic are kept up to date as new transactions are received. Most modern predictive analytic and machine learning platforms make it easy to deploy models as APIs for use in this way.

- Database scoring, perhaps the most traditional approach, involves running the predictive analytic model in a batch mode so that the resulting score is available in the database and can be passed into the Decision Service as part of its Input Data. This is easy to do and widely used, but it results in scores that could be out of date when accessed in fast moving situations.

- Some predictive analytic models can be represented as business rules or as functions within a BRMS. This can be achieved through manual or automatic import of models (using PMML for instance) to create rules and rule artifacts that are executable.
- Predictive analytic models can be executed natively by generating code or SQL for the model that the Decision Service can call when the result of the predictive analytic model is needed.

Build Business Rules or Decision Logic

Rules-based decisions consist of a set of business rules or decision logic that should be evaluated and executed as a set. Some sets of business rules may need to be executed before others. This is defined by the decision dependency model and implemented as decision flow. The rules implementing a single decision in the model are a single unit. Reuse of business rules or decision logic is generally at the sub-decision level. It is decisions for which access control, security policies, and governance approaches should be defined.

Just as using machine learning to develop predictive analytic models has some benefits, so too does representing decisions as business rules. Writing business rules can avoid the training overhead inherent in machine learning. Business rules can also be written for scenarios where no historical data exists. Capturing business rules engages business experts more fully, helping with organizational change and serving to capture a human perspective on the company's historical experience. Business rules-based decisions can also be balanced against those using machine learning to increase the robustness of the overall decision.

Building a set of business rules or decision logic for a decision used in a Decision Service involves defining business rules based on the decision logic requirements discovered earlier and integrating the business rules as part of the Decision Service.

Define Business Rules

Business rules are supported by software products known as Business Rules Management Systems (BRMS) or, sometimes, Decision Management Systems (DMS). A BRMS or DMS stores the business rules in a rule repository and provides tooling to allow you to author, manage, test, verify, simulate and deploy the business rules you develop.

A business rule consists of a set of conditions that check the values of attributes defined in the objects available to the Decision Service, and one or more actions to take or consequences to enforce if all those conditions are true. The actions are defined in terms of the answers allowed for the decision the business rules are implementing. These values are stored in specific attributes available to the Decision Service, either temporary ones of use only within the Decision Service or those defined as part of its output. Business rules might also have a name, a description, and other metadata such as owners or version history to assist in ongoing management.

How to effectively develop business rules for a real project could fill a book on its own, and if you look at the bibliography you can find several excellent references. At a high level, four steps are at the heart of developing business rules: selecting representations, writing the rules themselves, linking to sources, and validating that the rules are correct.

Select Business Rules Representation

Many BRMS offer multiple business rule representation, or ways to manage business rules. Some BRMS specialize in specific representations or use a single representation in all circumstances. Given your choice of BRMS, you will have to choose from one or more representations for business rules each time you author a rule set.

Keep an open mind about representation

Keep an open mind about which representation will make the most sense for each set of business rules. Each set will have different volatility and update frequencies, for instance. This information is part of the analysis of decisions and will help guide the right representation choice for a rule set. Most organizations find that they need to use different representations or to use the same representation in quite different ways for different rule sets.

The major representation approaches are as follows:

- **Decision Table**: By far the most common representation of decision logic or business rules. In a decision table each row is a rule. Condition and action columns are defined each containing an attribute. A rule is specified by putting values in the columns that map to the conditions of the rule and putting the consequences in the action columns to show the actions to be taken. More complex rules can be written by adding more columns. Because the rules that implement a sub-decision often have a similar structure, this can be a very effective representation for managing business rules. Sometimes the rows and columns are reversed with each column representing a business rule and each row representing a condition or action.

- **Decision Tree**: A decision tree represents a set of business rules using a branching format. A decision tree consists of a set of linked nodes where each node is a condition and has multiple branches from it, each representing a possible outcome of the condition. The final layer of the tree is a set of action definitions. Every path from the first or root node to each end action corresponds to one rule. These rules have the same root node—they share a condition—and each group will have one or more additional layers of shared nodes. Decision trees work well when groups of rules in a rule set share some, but not all, conditions—they are not symmetric.

Friendly Enough Expression Language (FEEL)

The DMN standard contains a definition of an expression language for business rules. This is "friendly enough" to be used by business people while still being precise and executable. Several modeling tools and some BRMS products support FEEL as a way to specify logic, more support it as a way to interchange logic.

- **Freeform Rules**: The simplest representation is one that simply allows a set of business rules to be written one after another in a list. Each rule can use any available attributes in its conditions and there is no requirement for the consequences of the various rules to be similar. Each BRMS has its own syntax for freeform rules. Many have a syntax that is "English-like," and most are extremely readable, allowing less technical users to read and write business rules without interpretation from IT staff.

- **Graphs**: While not very widespread, some BRMS support a graph format for representing business rules. While similar to a decision tree, they allow nodes to be reused, resulting in a more compact format.

Templates

Many BRMS allow templates to be defined for some or all of the representations they support. Templates typically allow some parts of the rules in the representation to be changed and may allow rules to be added or removed in controlled ways. For instance, a freeform rule template may allow the values in the conditions for a rule to be changed while not allowing the rule to be deleted or its action to be redefined. A decision tree template may allow new branches to be added while restricting the user to the set of actions already defined.

Templates can make it easier to support less technically capable rule writers. By reducing the scope of changes and supporting the author with pre-defined values or selections, syntactic errors can be largely or even wholly eliminated.

Write Business Rules

Once a representation has been selected for the business rules in a decision, an initial set of business rules needs to be developed. These need to implement the decision logic requirements identified and support the test cases defined earlier. In addition, they must conform to the overall contract of the Decision Service. Each sub decision implemented with business rules must also confirm to its own set of allowable answers. It must not be possible for the business rules written to return an answer not included in the list of answers. All the business rules must result in one of the allowed answer for the decision the rule set represents.

As well as producing the allowed answers, the rules in a decision must often explain how the answer was arrived at. Sometimes this is self-evident from the action taken, especially if there are multiple rules that result in the same answer. It is often useful to return supporting information, messages and annotations to explain the answer selected.

For instance, multiple rules might identify a policy as invalid but provide different messages and annotations to explain the specific reason why. These messages and annotations are not used by other decisions as inputs but can be collected and presented to a user or stored for audit purposes.

Business rules from data mining and machine learning

Provided that the attributes used by the rules, created using data mining or machine learning techniques, are available within the data model of your BRMS, then re-creating the rules created by data mining within the BRMS is trivial. The business rules found through data mining are typically close to, if not actually, executable business rules. These business rules can be created either manually or automatically by importing Predictive Model Markup Language or PMML (an XML representation of a predictive analytic model).

However, a manual process has now been introduced into the deployment of the Decision Service. As the data mining or machine learning results change (and they will, as customer behavior changes) the rules will have to be re-created within the BRMS. A manual process can increase the time it takes to deploy updates to the Decision Service and introduces a step where human error can cause inaccuracies.

Decision logic requirements do not generally refer to the actual objects that exist in the systems with which a Decision Service will be integrated. Business rules, on the other hand, must execute against these objects—they must be able to manipulate the objects that exist in the rest of your information systems. The business rules will often use a mapping layer so that the user sees a rule described in business terms but the rules execute against the detailed executable object model defined for the Decision Service.

Link to Knowledge Sources

The ability to find and change rules as circumstances change is much more important for success in Digital Decisioning than the ability to rapidly execute business rules. It is important that the initial version of the business rules is accurate and that it executes rapidly and effectively.

Many business rules are volatile, and there is often the potential for external drivers to cause change in business rules. As a result, managing the business rules— identifying the rules that must change, finding those rules, and accurately changing them—is often more important for long term project success.

Making sure that all business rules are the implementation of a known decision in a decision model is essential. It is also useful to keep links between the Knowledge Sources from which rules are derived and the business rules themselves . This is generally done at the decision level but a more fine grained linkage of Knowledge Source paragraphs to specific business rules may be necessary in a few cases.

Traceability of business rules

Many BRMS allow you to extend the repository to keep track of additional information. You are strongly urged to do so. Maintaining links from the business rules you can change in a BRMS to the decisions those rules support will make it much easier to manage change. Traceability from Knowledge Sources to the decisions the rules execute also makes it easier to find, scope, and manage the changes you will need to make to your business rules.

With these links in place, it will be easier to do impact analysis. It will be possible to see which business rules will need to be changed based on a change to a particular policy or regulation. It will be easier to find the business rules that must be changed when a best practice changes. When looking at a specific set of business rules it will be possible to tell which decisions are impacted directly or indirectly. All this helps business users manage change.

Validate and Verify

Each set of rules should be validated, verified, and tested as a unit in addition to being tested as part of the Decision Service. Many decisions are reused in a decision model, and it is a best practice to maximize such reuse and manage the implementation of those reused decisions appropriately.

1. Validate that all the business rules have been written in a valid way. They should use the correct syntax, only refer to objects

and attributes that exist, use valid comparators (no comparing numbers to strings, for instance), and more. This is typically either enforced by the editor in the BRMS or easy to check using an automated routine.

2. Verify the business rules. This involves focusing on the rule set or a group of rule sets in a decision flow and verifying that it is complete and correct by examining the structure of the rules. For instance, if a rule set is expected to set a particular attribute, and it is known that the attribute can have one of five values, the rule set can be verified by checking that each value is at least possible given the rules. Similarly, if numeric ranges are being checked, then the rules can be verified to ensure that there are no potentially confusing overlaps or gaps in the ranges tested. There are many other tests, and each BRMS implements its own.

3. While it is possible to verify the accuracy of a rule set in structural terms, it will typically also be necessary to verify that it behaves correctly by developing and running tests. These are akin to unit test cases developed for pieces of code, and most BRMS manage and run these tests once they have been defined.

Use Simulation to Verify

Ongoing change of a Decision Service will require simulation capabilities as noted below. These simulation capabilities are primarily designed to show the business impact of a change. They can also be used during initial development to ensure that rules that are based on best practices and policy behave reasonably before they are deployed.

Build Optimization Models

There are three main use cases for optimization in Digital Decisioning:

- **Optimization within a single decision**
  Optimization can be used within a single decision to optimize its response based on information about the single transaction for which a decision is required. In this case, an optimization model represents a decision in the decision model.

- **Optimization across many decisions**

When batches of decisions are being made, optimization can be used to optimize the decisions being made by considering all the transactions as a set. This would show up as a decision only when a set of decisions are being compared or integrated.

- **Optimization of future decision-making approaches**
  Finally, once decisions have been made, optimization can be used to analyze historical results and optimize the way decisions should be made in the future—essentially optimizing the logic of the decisions rather than the decisions themselves. This third option is discussed in Chapter 7 as part of monitoring and improving decisions.

Optimization in a single decision

When a decision has a single, simple action such as an offer to be made to a customer, it is likely that optimization will need to be applied to a batch of such transactions. It makes sense, for instance, to consider what offers might be made to a group of customers to optimally allocate limited high-value offers where they will have the most business impact. If a single customer is being considered each time and only a simple action being determined, it is unlikely that optimization will make sense within the Decision Service.

When the action is a complex one, however, optimization may well be very effective inside a Decision Service for a single transaction. If the desired output is "present a feasible configuration of a product for this customer, minimizing cost" then the decision will involve a whole set of configuration parameters and options. Optimization may well be powerful or even necessary to generate the optimal solution in this case.

Optimization in this context refers to mathematical optimization or constraint programming. In both these approaches, an optimization model is a mathematical model that defines a problem. The model is typically defined as

1. A set of *decision variables* which represent the choices to be made.

2. An objective or measure of success.

3. A set of constraints defining what is allowable.

Once crafted, an optimization model can be instantiated with data, and a solver is then used to find possible solutions or the best possible (optimal) solution for the defined problem—a set of values for the decision variables that satisfies the constraints and meets or maximizes the objective.

Optimization can help find the balance between conflicting trade-offs or the most effective way to use a set of resources. Depending on the context, the resources you optimize might be capital and risk (in financial investment), physical space (transportation, warehousing, retail space planning), machine capacity (manufacturing planning and scheduling), or labor cost (workforce scheduling). Many optimization problems will naturally consider a combination of resource constraints and objectives.

The process of building mathematical optimization models has similarities with its machine learning counterpart, but there are a few major differences worth highlighting to avoid confusion:

- While predictive analytic models are *generated* by applying a machine learning algorithm to a data set, an optimization model is *formulated* by hand to represent a business problem by defining the decision variables, the objective, and the constraints.

- While the scope of data input to a machine learning algorithm is often relatively small (such as information about a customer), the scope of an optimization model is usually a complex transaction or a set of transactions.

- Machine learning algorithms generally require access to large amounts of historical data that can be used to train the model. Optimization models can be run against historical data but do not require it.

- While *invoking* a predictive model in a Decision Service is relatively fast and simple—it simply involves evaluating a formula or interpreting a decision tree—*solving* an optimization model can consume significant time and memory, depending on the complexity of the model and size of the data. The optimization model must search a large set of possible actions to determine the one that best fits the constraints and goals.

Optimization is well established in supply chain problem domains where it is often used to manage sourcing, manufacturing, distribution, and pricing. It might be used, for instance, to define which products to make on which machines in a factory to maximize the value of products produced given restricted access to the various machines needed to make the products. Scheduling is another common problem, where constraints include the need for workers with specific skills to be available at certain times while meeting requirements on working hours, shifts and safety. Similarly, your airplane seat, rental car, and hotel room are all likely to be priced using optimization technology.

Optimization models can be complex

Once again, the purpose of this section is to give an overview of how to use optimization in the context of Decision Services, not to define a complete methodology for doing so.

Define Decision Variables

The first step in building an optimization model is to define what you're trying to decide; i.e. the output of the model. A decision variable can be either a true/false variable (such as modeling whether an activity is happening in a certain time slot or not), an integer (such as deciding the placement of an item in time or space), or a rational or linear variable (such as representing the required quantity of a raw material). This will have been identified as the allowed answers for the decision being implemented. The type of variables used in a model determines the type of the model and the algorithm used to solve it—linear programming, (mixed) integer programming, or constraint programming, for example. These variables will be part of the data being manipulated by the Decision Service and will be the information requirements for the sub decision being implemented.

Define Objective

The second step in building an optimization model is to define its objective—what you wish to optimize. The objective is defined in terms of the decision variables and data, and calculates something that can either be maximized (or minimized) or defines a valid solution to a problem. The function defines what it is that you find valuable. This should be determined using the performance metrics and business objectives linked to the decision model.

For instance, an optimization problem might be trying to decide how to fit an order on to the cheapest possible set of delivery trucks. The function would define the cost of using various delivery trucks so that the total cost of any given solution to the decision problem could be calculated. Sometimes the goal is simply to find a solution that does not violate any constraints, and in this case there is no objective defined.

Define Constraints

The third and final element of the definition of an optimization problem is the set of constraints. This might define a limit on how many of something are available or might state that the value of one element of the solution must be greater than another value. In a scheduling problem, constraints might define which activities must be performed before another activity or which resources can perform a particular activity. In an allocation problem, it might define how much of a particular product can go on a particular truck, which kinds of trucks can carry which products or might limit which products can share a truck.

Constraints are typically divided into hard constraints and soft constraints. Hard constraints cannot be broken by a proposed solution. If no solution can be found that does not break a hard constraint, then the problem is overly constrained. Soft constraints can be broken, but a solution will be considered "better" the fewer such constraints it breaks. Sometimes soft constraints have a penalty value associated with them; this is used to reduce the objective value of a candidate solution if it breaks that constraint. For example, a scheduling problem might define "no one can be assigned to two shifts that overlap" as a hard constraint while "no one should be assigned to two shifts in a 20 hour period" might be a soft constraint with a penalty.

Some constraints are Input Data to the decision model, but many are decided by sub-decisions. For instance, a decision might identify that a power plant is available for a specific date. Many such decisions are made about all possible power plants to identify the set of power plants that should be considered for a supply optimization decision that must decide on the best mix of power plants to meet a forecasted need (with the forecast being another decision).

Building on business rules

Optimization technology is often used when an approach focused on using business rules has reached a point of diminishing returns. When there are very large numbers of business rules or when those business rules must be constantly traded off against one another so that the minimum number are violated, a business rules based Decision Service may not be effective or even practical. The rules developed up to that point are often a good basis for the definition of the constraints that an optimization system will need.

Some solutions also combine business rules and optimization more tightly than simply executing them sequentially in a Decision Service. A set of business rules can be defined where the actions of those rules configure an optimization problem. Different data will cause the business rules to take different actions and configure a slightly different optimization problem.

Constraints often look a lot like the condition part of a business rule. Instead of defining the action to be taken when a set of conditions are true, a constraint simply states a set of conditions that must be true. Some optimization systems even share a condition evaluation engine with a business rules management system.

Solve

The final step is to solve the optimization problem using an engine known as a solver. The solver will use the data available in the Decision Service and then find the best possible solution to the objective. Typically, a variety of mathematical techniques can be used either singly or in combination. The solver will evaluate large numbers of potential solutions and use the degree to which the objective is met and the constraints violated to hone in on the best possible solution to the problem. If the problem has more than one solution that does not violate the constraints, the solver can be configured either to seek the best of the viable solutions or simply to return the first one that doesn't violate the defined constraints.

The output of the solver is a set of values for the decision variables defined in the model, and thus defines the objective value of the solution as well as the feasibility and penalties of any soft constraints. These values might represent the actions that should be returned by the Decision Service or they might be input to further decisions in the decision flow.

Iterate as Needed

Decision Services are rarely complete when they are first deployed. Even when they are, the likelihood is that changing circumstances will cause regular and perhaps constant change to the decision-making approach used. An iterative development approach (in which the business rules for each sub-decision and the predictive analytic and optimization models used are developed incrementally) is much to be preferred over a waterfall approach.

Optimizing with predictions

One of the interesting areas for optimization is using predictive analytic models as inputs. For instance, optimization is often used to schedule pick up or delivery routes. When scheduling pick-ups one option is simply to use the pick-ups requested so far and re-optimize the remaining pick-ups during the day. As each new pick-up is called in, the schedule is revised. However, this could result in trucks being badly out of position if a sequence of pick-ups gets requested in one part of town.

It is possible to use predictive analytics to address this. Data about previous days could be used to generate the likelihood that a pick-up will be called in today for each part of town – this would be another decision in the model. As pick-ups are called in, this information can be combined with information about the likelihood of additional pick-ups in the future to optimize the schedule based on what has already happened and what is likely to happen later.

The decision model provides a useful frame for identifying iterations because specific sub-decisions can be stubbed out initially, providing only a generic or "not known" response. These decisions can be fleshed out in subsequent iterations. The decision model allows pieces to be identified and implemented without losing track of the overall problem to be solved.

Build Decision Management Environment

Build Decision Monitoring Environment

The ongoing performance of a Decision Service will need to be monitored so that the business can track the success and effectiveness of the decisions involved. In addition, IT will want to monitor the performance characteristics of the Decision Service (response times, issues with timeouts, other failed requests, etc.). Monitoring will also help identify ways to make ongoing improvements on how decisions are being made. A suitable decision monitoring environment will need to be built that has access to data about decision performance, as well as links to the overall business performance management environment.

Monitor effectiveness and approach

Many of the drivers for change in a Decision Service can be monitored using an environment like this, but not all. Regulations and policies that impact the Decision Service should also be monitored for changes that might require a change in decision-making approach.

A decision monitoring environment presents data that can be used to assess the performance and effectiveness of the Decision Service as well as data about how the decision was made. Various reporting and analysis tools are made available so that business owners can see what changes might make sense. Business Intelligence solutions that provide dashboards and reports are ideal for building the basics of a decision monitoring environment. Business users and IT are typically very familiar with them, and they offer enough flexibility that users with different goals can be given custom views of the information that reflect what they are interested in.

Reporting facilities involve both pre-defined reports on the performance and effectiveness of a Decision Service, and ad-hoc query and reporting to allow the owner of a Decision Service to investigate its performance in new ways. All Decision Services should support reports or dashboards that show:

- The distribution of outcomes in a time period to see how the overall decision is varying.
- The specific values of each sub-decision for each transaction or group of transactions so that sub-decisions that need change can be identified.
- The distribution of critical values in the Input Data to see if the transactions being handled are changing.

Decision Services might also provide reports that are more specific to the particular decision being made. For instance, a report comparing the cost of retention offers accepted in a particular period with the predicted value of those customers who accepted offers during that period.

While many Decision Services can be effectively monitored by regularly reviewing reports, it is likely to be more effective to set up monitoring and alerting facilities. Business users responsible for several Decision Services might find overall dashboards effective. A Marketing Manager, for instance, might want a dashboard that summarizes the performance of the cross-sell, up-sell, retention, and acquisition Decision Services.

Reporting and monitoring best practices still apply

All of the best practices you have developed for building a reporting and monitoring environment apply to decision monitoring. The purpose of this environment is to enable business owners to make decisions about decisions—to make the tactical decisions about how to change the decision-making approaches for their operational decisions.

Alerts can also be defined based on performance of the Decision Service that is either out of acceptable bounds, different from recent results, or otherwise exceptional. As for reporting, some of this could be defined for a Decision Service independent of its purpose. Thus, an alert could be defined for any Decision Service if the distribution of results in the last 5 days was different from the last 30 in some statistically significant way. More usefully, each Decision Service has specific situations that are noteworthy such as sudden changes in offer acceptance rates or hitting a particular target for fraud in a month.

Link Performance Metrics and Decision Management

When conducting decision discovery, all top-level decisions were mapped to key performance indicators (KPIs) or metrics. This linkage helps ensure that all decisions are discovered and gives a basis for assessing Decision Service performance. If we know which decisions support which objectives and measures, we can make assumptions about the Decision Services that implement those decisions. If a Decision Service makes a decision that moves the associated metrics in a positive direction, it can be considered a "good decision." Our understanding of the metrics and objectives enables us to understand the difference between good decisions and bad decisions made by a Decision Service. This linkage allows us to track the effectiveness of decision making just like anything else in our performance management environment. We can track not only our financial performance but also our decision performance.

When developing the decision monitoring environment, give some thought to the way in which decision performance and business performance relate. An integrated approach to decision and business performance monitoring will make it easier to improve the decisions and so improve business results.

Build Rule Management Environment

By far the most common change that will be required as part of ongoing decision monitoring and improvement will be a change to business rules. Business rules will have to be changed when regulations or policies change as well as when the underlying data being used to make a decision changes. Any new decision-making approach for A/B or champion-challenger testing will involve new or at least modified business rules. Therefore, you should invest in creating a rule management environment designed for business experts.

The use of a BRMS or DMS makes the logic of a Decision Service much more accessible for non-technical business experts than traditional code-based approaches. Graphical business rules representations such as decision tables and the natural-language like approach of a typical BRMS, combined with a suitable executable object model, make it possible for IT and business experts to collaborate effectively on the business rules. Whether the business experts code the rules themselves or rely on business analysts or IT professionals is less important than this ability to collaborate when defining the bulk of the business rules a Decision Service needs.

When a Decision Service has high volatility, however, and business rules changes must be made regularly, the situation is different. When the need to make a rapid business rules change is a common one, or when large numbers of business rules must be changed periodically, the value of having the business experts make the change themselves increases. The best way to support the decision monitoring and improvement phase for these kinds of Decision Services will be to create a business-centric rules management environment.

A business-centric rules management environment has a number of characteristics:

- **Each business expert sees only the business rules for which they are responsible**: Multiple business experts might use the rule management environment, and they should be able to read those rules they have read permissions for and change those rules they have read/wrote permissions for. They should not have to navigate through a lot of other rules or rule repository structures to find them.

- **These business rules are presented in context:** Business users are making these changes in a decision context—for instance, they are changing sub-decisions in response to new regulations or trying to improve the performance of the Decision Service by changing a specific sub-decision. This context should be reflected in the rule management environment so that changing the rules feels like just part of running the business.

- **The business rules editing environment allows only those changes that make sense:** Some rules can only be changed in certain ways because of the underlying data—only certain values can be set as a consequence of a rule for instance.

Conditions and consequences that make no business or technical sense should not be allowed. If the overall Decision Service constrains the specific rules in question to behave within a range of allowed behavior, then this should also be enforced.

- **The business expert can rapidly see the impact of their proposed changes**: The rule management environment should be linked to the impact analysis tools and techniques described below.

- **No unnecessary technical information is presented:** With an environment like this, the business experts can take more direct control over the business rules changes that are required. This will reduce the time to make the changes and improve their accuracy by eliminating the impedance of a business/IT hand off.

Build Model Management Environment

Predictive analytic models and other algorithms, whether built using traditional predictive analytic techniques, machine learning or using AI, age and degrade over time. MLOps has become established as a practice post deployment. MLOps ensures that machine learning and other analytic models continue to run effectively once deployed. An argument could be made for building a business user focused environment that allows management of analytic models. In practice this has not yet become a mainstream proposition. Vendors are making it easier for less technical people to build models. The idea of a distinct management environment for ongoing evolution and maintenance has not gained much traction. What is agreed to be essential, however, is an environment for managing and tracking the performance of these models.

An analytic model management environment should allow a non-technical user to review the effectiveness of a model, changes in its precision such as increases in false positive rates, and changes in the distribution of answers such as more high risk scores as a percentage of all scores generated. These changes may impact the decisions being made using the analytics and might require that the models be updated.

When modern machine learning platforms are used, models may be updated continually. In these situations, business users will want to be alerted to new versions that are noticeably different from previous ones or that vary in novel ways from previous versions. They may also be interested in knowing that the pace of change has increased or decreased. The specifics will vary with the degree of automation in model updates but business users need to be able to see what is changing, what's driving the change and the impact on decision-making of that change.

Integrate Decision Services

Once built, Decision Services need to be integrated with the rest of the information technology environment of which they will be part. Data must be passed to the Decision Service so that it can process transactions, and data must be captured when it is returned from the Decision Service so that it can be acted upon. The Decision Service must be integrated with the business processes and event-based systems that need it. Many Decision Services do not handle 100% of transactions, so it is also worth considering how a Decision Service can be integrated with Case Management systems.

Deploy and Integrate Continuously

If you begin by defining the Decision Service contract and test cases, it should be possible to immediately integrate the "empty" Decision Service. This mean that each new set of business rules, modifications to existing business rules, new or updated analytic or machine learning models can be deployed and integrated with your other systems and processes immediately. A continuous process to deploy and integrate changes to your Decision Service as you develop them is highly recommended.

A continuous integration and deployment process ensures that each new or updated sub-decision works and can be used. It also supports the kind of iterative development that works best for Digital Decisioning. With a continuous deployment approach, each update will be available to the Decision Service quickly and will improve the running Decision Service immediately, whether it is running in production or only in a development/testing environment. Because these changes are contained within the Decision Service, they will not require re-integration as the scaffolding will remain the same.

Data Integration

Decision Services vary in the extent to which they gather their own data once they have been invoked. Calls to Decision Services pass some data that will be used as the basis for the decision returned by the service. This is simple when the calling systems all have the information that the Decision Service requires. It becomes more complex for decisions that might require large amounts of data or where the calling context varies a great deal. At one extreme are Decision Services that must be passed all the data they require. At the other extreme are Decision Services in which even long running requests for data, say those involving a human, can be accommodated.

Four broad options for data in Decision Service exist:

1. Pass all the data available into a Decision Service and force it to either decide or to pass back some reason why it could not, so that the calling application can assemble any additional data required and try again.

   The most "pure" kind of Decision Service, this approach is simple and fast. It can result in multiple attempts to get a decision more often than other options. It lends itself to remote operation because it needs no data access of its own. It can also result in calling applications investing time in collecting data that may or may not be relevant to the decision itself; this can be a problem when some data is only required occasionally.

Business processes can assemble data

When a business process management system is going to be calling Decision Services, the assembly of data to pass to the Decision Service is rarely a problem. Business process management systems are well equipped when it comes to getting data from multiple systems, assembling it into a coherent package of data, and passing it to a service. This allows the Decision Service to be defined to expect a broad set of data. Even when multiple legacy systems are the source of the data, Robotic Process Automation of RPA tools can greatly assist.

---

2. Pass the data available to the Decision Service but allow it to

make synchronous calls to external services and databases to gather the data it needs to complete the decision.

This approach can be particularly useful when the Decision Service involves machine learning models. These often change regularly and require new calculated attributes to be passed to them at execution time. These calculated attributes can often be maintained in an analytic environment that takes advantage of streaming technology to update aggregates, calculations, averages and time series as each new transaction is received. When the service calls out to the model the required data can be retrieved from the streaming environment. This allows the core Decision Service to maintain a stable contract even as the machine learning model needs new attributes.

Regardless of the specifics, the Decision Service must handle timeouts, and it must degrade gracefully if these additional data sources are not available. This approach is also fairly fast and simple. It can also allow costly or time consuming requests for information to be deferred until and unless they are required. It does make the Decision Service dependent on other components, however.

3. Pass the data available to the Decision Service and allow it to gather the data it needs in any way.

The Decision Service may need to be put "on ice" while waiting for data. The Decision Service can no longer be used in a real-time or interactive context as it cannot be relied upon to make a decision in a reasonable time. It should be invoked asynchronously, gather the data it needs, and then transmit its result, typically as an event. This approach is better suited to event-based architectures.

4. Pass the data available to the Decision Service, and allow it to request additional data from a user interface.

This might involve a customer (such as someone applying for insurance) or an employee (entering additional data required by a process). The decision continues to run until the data is provided through the user interface or the request for a decision is cancelled. These Decision Services usually require a definition of the decision and an additional set of business rules to handle the interaction, display the correct questions, and adapt the user interface to gather the required data.

Good Decision Service design requires a clear understanding of what is needed from a requirements perspective and plausible from an architectural and technical perspective. Option 1 is the most pure and most common, but can be limiting when large amounts of data are involved. Option 2 is effective when data is expensive and when machine learning models are an integral part of the Decision Services. Options 3 and 4 provide more flexibility but increase the challenges: coupling increases as does the number of failure points, which can be crippling if not managed well. The complexity can rapidly increase because of maintenance, monitoring, and error handling needs, and more resources must be dedicated to manage the additional integration points in the infrastructure.

A hybrid approach can be useful

One of the most common hybrid approaches is to break a Decision Service into two parts. One determines what data is needed to make a decision in a particular case while the other makes the decision once the relevant data has been collected. For instance, the first might decide if a motor vehicle report is needed to process a particular applicant for insurance while the second uses that data as part of the underwriting decision. These share many sub-decisions to ensure they are coherent and aligned.

Process Integration

Integrating a business process with a Decision Service is generally very straightforward. The business process will generally collect up all the information needed by the Decision Service, accessing whatever range of systems are involved. This data is then passed as a package to the Decision Service using a standard service call for the environment— generally a web services invocation. The Decision Service runs and returns the result like any other service, and the process continues. Handling time outs and other mechanical issues is built into the process design as it would be for any other service call.

BPMN, CMMN and DMN

It is common to use Business Process Model and Notation (BPMN) and Case Management Model and Notation (CMMN) with DMN when integrating with business process and case management environments. The two approaches are compatible with DMN and the standards are easy to use together. At the time of writing the formal integration of the notation has not been codified. A common sense approach that links tasks to specific decisions that are exposed in Decision Services works well and allows for easy mapping of the process or case data to the decisions' inputs.

Processes that use a Decision Service often have worklists or case management steps to handle those transactions where the service could not make a decision. As a result, it is common to see a branch immediately after the call to the Decision Service. This will contain one or more branches for those transactions where the decision was made as well as one that routes the transaction to a worklist or a case management environment. Where the Decision Service was selecting a particular approach, such as one determining if a claim should be fast tracked or referred for fraud investigation, each action will have its own branch and a set of process steps or a sub-process that is appropriate to that option.

Event Integration

Integrating a Decision Service with an event-based system is even simpler. The Decision Service is set up with a listener for the events that contain information about a transaction that must be processed by the Decision Service. When such an event is detected, the Decision Service or Decision Agent executes and makes a decision. Depending on the action, it then puts the relevant action event back on the event bus so that other systems can handle it.

The Decision Service can be passed only the event instance and the data associated with it or it can be passed the entire collection of events whose correlation triggered the need for the decision in the first place. Sometimes the decision being made is an assessment of the need to trigger a new event. For instance, does the pattern of events warrant a fraud investigation? In this case the whole sequence of events might be passed to a Decision Service that decides if an "Investigate" event is called for.

Sometimes event and process integration are combined. A Decision Service may be triggered by an event and then kick off a business process to handle the decision action. Similarly a Decision Service may be called from a business process and may result in additional events being generated that will be put onto an event bus in parallel with the rest of the process continuing to execute.

Case Management Integration

Case management systems are often integrated with Digital Decisioning. Many Digital Decisioning scenarios cannot make decisions in 100% of transactions, and often the remaining transactions are considered cases that must be managed through a manual decision-making process. This is generally only true for relatively high-value decisions. For instance, a Decision Service that makes commercial underwriting decisions would likely put any application for insurance that it could not process into a case management system for an underwriter to review. Even if a Decision Service can make a decision, it may still need to push that transaction into a case management environment. For instance, an organization may decide to manually review a certain randomly selected percentage of automated decisions. One of the most effective ways to do this is to push the information about the transaction and the decision made into a case management system. The simplest way to integrate a Decision Service and a case management system is simply to hand-off transactions that come back from the Decision Service as undecided or as flagged for review. As far as the Decision Service is concerned, that transaction is now dealt with and it will not see it again.

In the case of undecided transactions, however, the best practice is to consider the case management system as an integral part of the Digital Decisioning solution. When the Decision Service cannot decide about a transaction, it is generally because there is some assessment or judgment called for that requires human intervention. Instead of simply "giving up" on the transaction at this point the Decision Service could put a much more specific request into the case management system. This request could identify specific sub-decision for which a human intervention is needed, such as a visit to a commercial location to do an inspection. The case management system manages these requests before returning the data that results – the answers – to the Decision Service by re-invoking it with the new data. This more focused approach to using the case management system avoids the situation where a transaction that was *almost* suitable for automated decisioning is processed completely manually. Instead the Decision Service uses the case management system to gather additional data it needs so that it can, in the end, make a decision.

7. Monitor & Improve Decisions

A typical IT project ends when a system is complete, installed, and running as expected. Future changes are considered maintenance work and require a change order that feeds into a process for starting new IT projects to make the change. This is unacceptable for Decision Services.

First, because decision-making is more volatile than most other aspects of business being automated, change is likely to be greater and more rapid. Having to engage in a formal IT process for every change is likely to become burdensome and failing to make needed changes will reduce the value of the Decision Service over time. Second, it is often necessary to gather data and conduct experiments to see what decision-making approaches might be effective. Changes to the Decision Service will be required to implement any conclusions.

Once a Decision Service is deployed, it should be monitored and improved. The most successful are those that can be readily updated and modified by the line of business—the people who own the problem being addressed.

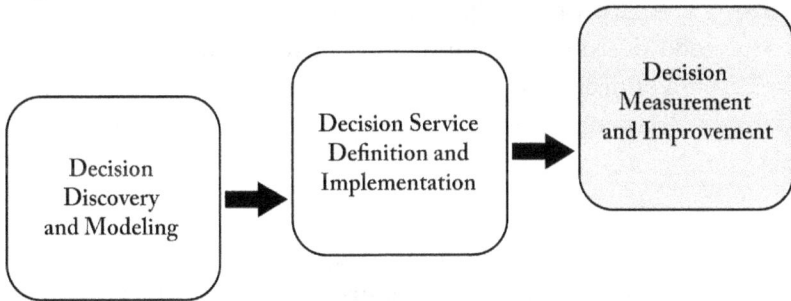

Figure 7-1 Decision Measurement and Improvement in Context

Decisions should be analyzed before deployment

This chapter is primarily concerned with the monitoring and improvement of decisions once the Decision Service has been deployed. Many of these techniques and approaches should also be used prior to deploying the initial version of the Decision Service. What-if analysis, simulation and more are all useful for ensuring that a new Decision Service will behave as expected.

Monitor For Changes

Many changes to decision-making approaches are driven by explicit change and are reactive. The goals and key performance indicators or metrics of your business set a context that defines what a good or an effective decision looks like. Regulations and policies constrain how decisions are made. Your Decision Services must respond to changes in this business context.

It is also important to be able to make proactive changes. Periodic analysis of the effectiveness of the decisions being made by a Decision Service can identify opportunities for proactive changes to improve decision-making effectiveness. You may not have implemented the most effective decision-making approach initially but monitoring decision performance will allow you to eliminate responses that have bad outcomes.

To effectively monitor decisions, you need to capture data about decision effectiveness, track policy and regulatory changes, monitor business goals and be aware of changes in your underlying data.

Capture Decision Effectiveness Data

Any good decision monitoring system will require data about the effectiveness of decisions to be collected. Three main kinds of data are involved—decision execution data, response data and general business data.

Decision Execution Data:

As a Decision Service executes, it can record what decision was requested and what answer was returned through which interaction point. It can include a timestamp and a unique identifier, allowing it to be tied back to the subject of the decision—a specific customer or account, for example. This baseline information is essential for tracking decision effectiveness.

A Decision Service can record a wide range of additional execution information, which should be logged for analysis purposes. This includes:

- The outcome of every sub-decision in the model – the particular answer selected from that decision's set of allowed answers. Ideally, every sub-decision is made for every transaction and recorded. The sub-decision outcomes should be recorded in the structure of the decision model to support analysis.

- If a decision was implemented as a predictive analytic model or machine learning algorithm, the score or algorithm result can be recorded along with the explanation or reason codes generated by the algorithm. Many machine learning algorithms, and some more advanced predictive analytic approaches, result in opaque models. Leaving these as black boxes can be hard to sell to business owners and unacceptable in regulated environments. Some vendors are adding explanations to these models, enriching the value calculated with information on the key factors that influenced the result each time. In addition, various open source and commercial products exist that can generate plausible explanations of any algorithm, no matter how complex or unknown. Where more advanced algorithms are used in a Decision Service, integrate such explanations into the decision data captured.

- The decision-making approach that was used for a given transaction if more than one was designed in for A/B or Champion-Challenger testing. As noted above, it is preferable if all possible decisions are made and recorded for each transaction. This will allow the outcomes of all experiments to be accessible later in the process and so ensure consistency. The action taken will depend on the approach selected so the output data needs to record that information also.

You may be required (for audit and compliance requirements) to retain detailed logs in order to be able to precisely trace and audit any given decision. This includes the specific business rules executed for each sub-decision as well as the full set of data that was sent to the Decision Service. However, logging at this level may add a processing overhead on the Decision Service that needs to be traded against the need for auditing.

Decision Response Data

When a Decision Service makes a decision and this decision is acted on there will usually be some consequence for the recipient of the decision. For example, a customer being made a specific offer in real time may reject the offer, accept it, click on it for more information, defer it for another time, etc. It should be possible to collect this data at the time the decision was returned to the recipient and be able to tie it back to the specific decision execution data.

Assessing the effectiveness of the decision-making approach will require this information. For instance, if a customer retention offer is presented to a customer and that customer is retained, it will be important to know if they accepted the offer, ignored it, or considered it but did not in the end accept it. Without this information, it will be impossible to understand exactly what impact the offer had.

Decision Outcome Data

It will be likely that any useful monitoring system will need to incorporate information not directly generated by the Decision Service. Consider a Decision Service designed to make decisions about routing claims to a Fraud Investigator or not. Assessing the effectiveness of this decision will require a combination of data on which claims were referred by the Decision Service and which ones were later successfully identified to be fraudulent by the Fraud Investigators.

Being able to tie outcomes like this back to each individual decision is vital for the ongoing improvement of the system. It provides the round trip data required to refresh and improve any predictive models, and it gives insight into the performance of individual business rules.

Track Changes to Business Goals and Metrics

The way a Decision Service behaves is driven by your business goals. A decision's impact on those business goals determines if it is a good decision or a bad decision. This is measured using the metrics and key performance indicators you have established for tracking the progress of your business against those goals. Part of the model you have of your decisions is their linkage to these metrics and business goals.

When business goals or key performance indicators change, the behavior of the Decision Services related to that goal must also change. For instance, the metric for customer retention success could change from a flat percentage—retain a specific percentage of all customers at the end of their contract—to one that involves retaining only those customers who are or could become profitable. Such a change will alter the way customer retention offer decisions are made as well as other decisions that have an impact on customer retention.

It may also become apparent during operations that specific decisions should be linked to additional metrics and KPIs. For instance, a marketing manager might decide that an offer needs to be discontinued because the uptake for this offer has been so large that they are going to struggle to fulfill the requests. The offer was being accepted by around 500 people every day and was resulting in serious increases in wait times at the call center. The decision had been linked to the metrics for campaign effectiveness but not to the metrics for call center responsiveness. Once the decision was being made in production it became clear that this decision could have a negative impact on call center effectiveness. With the decision now linked to two sets of metrics the business objective changes from one of simply presenting a compelling offer to as many customers as possible to one that reflects the need for call center support. The marketing manager will need to change the Decision Service to deactivate this offer and replace it with one that requires less call center support. This level of agility is essential—waiting days for an IT change request will not allow the marketing manager to meet the changing business goal.

Identifying the need for this kind of reactive change requires that the decisions are linked to the metrics and key performance indicators of the business. This information needs to be up to date as metrics and business goals evolve. When business owners discuss changes to metrics and business goals, they can use this information to identify those decisions where a change might be required. In addition, when discussing the effectiveness of a Decision Service, they can review this information to see if it needs to be changed. Any change to the metrics linked to a decision should cause a reactive assessment of the decision-making approach(es) currently being used for that decision.

Identify New or Changed Regulations or Policies

Many decisions are dependent on regulations and policies to define how they should be made. When these regulations or policies change, or when new regulations or policies are issued that impact how a decision is made, the business rules implementing those decision will need to be updated. A new version of the Decision Services that implement those decisions will need to be deployed. For instance, an eligibility service implements a government regulation that specifies certain circumstances in which an organization must approve requests for service from consumers. A court case related to the regulation clarifies how it should be interpreted, changing the organization's eligibility rules. The legal team needs to be able to make a change to the Decision Service to reflect this new interpretation quickly and accurately both to avoid fines and to minimize the amount of re-work that would be required when people who were rejected under the old rules re-apply.

This requires an understanding of links between source regulations and policies, documented in the decision model as Knowledge Sources, and the Decisions dependent on them. A process for ensuring that changes to the regulations and policies defined in the decision inventory are highlighted in a timely fashion will allow the identification of the decisions where the decision-making approach will need to be evaluated to ensure it will remain compliant.

Some regulatory changes are immediate

Most regulation and policy changes are known about in advance. Most governments issue new regulations in advance of their effective date, and major company policies usually have an extended review process. This means that changes to decision-making approach can often be considered in advance with plenty of time to make the change. However, some changes are much more immediate, such as court rulings that interpret the meaning of a regulation or a policy change in response to a disaster or a problem at a competitor. These changes will need to be rapidly assessed and changes made almost instantly. You need to be prepared for both.

Track Changes to the Underlying Data

The most effective approach to a decision is often based on the analysis of historical data. Any Decision Service that uses predictive analytic models or machine learning algorithms or even business rules derived from data mining, is behaving the way it does because of the data that was analyzed. This data was analyzed at a point in time, however, and data recorded since then might reveal different patterns. Data changes mean that the result of this analysis can change also.

For instance, you may learn something new about the customer:

You're a mobile telecommunications company and you begin sending customers at risk of leaving marketing offers to tempt them to stay. Some accept these offers and stay, some ignore them but stay anyway, and some ignore them and leave. Once the offers start being made, you can see who accepts the offers and who does not. You start to collect data about offers accepted and offers ignored as well as about the effectiveness of these offers. You now have new data that can be used to drive better decisions in the future. This new knowledge about who did and who did not respond to this campaign should be used as input into the next round of modeling. The way in which future retention offers are selected may then be different.

You may also collect additional data: Obtaining access to new kinds of data is a common way to build better predictive analytic models using machine learning. Many projects start with structured data within the organization, such as transactional data. Over time they move on to data from outside the organization, such as demographic data. They may also start considering unstructured data, such as information typed into call center notes during interactions with the customer, or high-volume data such as weblogs that show the items looked at in the on-line store. Even social and attitudinal data, such as that from surveys, can be included. Each time you gain access to new data there is an opportunity to re-build and improve upon the predictive analytic models being used within the Decision Service.

Adding new algorithms

When new data sources are added, or new kinds of data become accessible, consider adding new algorithms to your decision model. There may well be areas of the decision made based on best practices or accumulated experience where a new machine learning algorithm could be used instead. Similarly, there may be decisions made a certain way because something is considered unknowable that may be estimated or predicted using new data and more advanced algorithms. Don't simply refine existing models with new data, look for new opportunities also.

Finally, people's behavior changes over time, and this is reflected in new data patterns. For instance, fraudsters are continuously looking for ways to defraud insurance companies. The pattern of data that shows something as fraudulent will therefore change as they try and outmaneuver your existing fraud detection approach. If you don't notice this, or if you cannot refresh your fraud Decision Service quickly, then there may be a significant number of new instances of fraud that the service does not automatically identify.

For example, there is a growing problem of staged car accidents where a well-organized criminal gang causes car accidents by purposefully braking hard in front of a distracted driver. They claim that they were not at fault and that they were rear-ended by the other driver. They make a claim for both car damage and expensive "injuries." You want your Decision Service to flag these new types of fraud as soon as you become aware of them.

Always monitor models once developed

Some data science teams take a "fire and forget" approach to developing predictive analytic models and applying machine learning algorithms. They do data analysis as part of developing the initial model but fail to monitor the model once developed. There may be no central repository of models that can be used to see how each model was developed. There may be no process for monitoring those data sources used to see if the data characteristics are changing.

This approach is unacceptable when developing predictive analytic models and algorithms for use in Decision Services. Accurate definitions of how models were built and ongoing monitoring of those models to see if a recalibration or a rebuild is appropriate is a necessity. Modern machine learning tools automate many of these tasks in the context of a specific analytic model. This automation should be combined with the decision context for maximum effectiveness.

Regular customer behavior also changes over time, with new trends and shifting markets and demographics being reflected in the data you collect about customer behavior. In all these cases, it will make sense to refresh machine learning algorithms as the data changes. The creation of new predictive analytic models will, in turn, cause new decisions to be made and new rules to be written.

Not all changes in data will require a change in decision making. Identifying those changes that merit a response requires an understanding of the data. You need to understand the data sources being used to make decisions as well as those being used to develop analytic models. You also need an environment that monitors the data used to develop analytic models and algorithms to see if its distribution has changed since the models were developed. This information and suitable analysis tools are available in most environments used to develop the predictive analytic models. A process is required for assessing new data sources to see if they would change the models developed and for reviewing the changing characteristics of the data sources used.

Determine the Response

Monitoring a Decision Service as well the business and regulatory environment in which it operates will identify the need for changes to the behavior of the Decision Service. Just because a change is needed does not automatically make it clear *what* change is needed. The specific drivers for change will need to be analyzed to see what change is required. The need for ongoing experimentation must also be assessed and a new approach or approaches designed.

The specific reasons why the behavior of a Decision Service must be changed can vary widely. A new regulation or policy may have been issued or an existing one updated. A court ruling or contract negotiation may have resulted in a new set of guidelines. Besides these external drivers, new data about customers and what they want may be available, or the behavior of customers may be shifting in response to market changes. Decision performance may also be an issue, either in terms of absolute performance or because a better approach has been proven.

Whatever the reason for the change, several elements must be analyzed to determine the appropriate change. Design time analysis based on the decision model implemented in the Decision Service may show what needs to be changed. Specific decision improvement opportunities may be identified. If multiple alternative approaches are being used in the Decision Service for either A/B testing or Champion-challenger testing, then the relative performance of these different approaches must be analyzed to see how to move forward most effectively.

Assess the Design Impact

The first step when deciding what change is going to be required is to conduct a design time impact analysis of the current Decision Service in the light of the change driver. The design of a Decision Service is based on a decision model showing everything involved in making a decision. This has been implemented as a decision flow or other execution sequence. This is supported by a contract that specifies the input and output data of the Decision Service. Each element is described either with a set of business rules or with a predictive analytic or optimization model. Because the Decision Service's behavior is driven by these explicitly modeled elements, it is possible to conduct detailed analysis and so design appropriate changes.

Technology for impact analysis

Conducting impact analysis generally involves using functionality built into your BRMS or DMS. If you are using a service repository or a master data management environment, these too can provide functionality for impact analysis.

Design impact analysis involves finding the artifacts (regulations, data, policies) that are changing and then navigating through the design to see what other elements of the Decision Service might also have to change. For instance, if a regulation has changed then design impact analysis can be used to list the decisions that are linked to the Knowledge Source representing the regulation. For each impacted decision, the analysis would list the business rules in those decisions that must be changed. In this way the scope of a potential regulatory change can be assessed in terms of the business rules that must be considered. Not all these business rules would need to change in most situations; the design impact analysis lists those with the potential to be impacted by the change.

Traceability is really important

Change is inevitable and systems for digital decisioning are among the highest change systems in your portfolio. It is important that your tools support the kind of traceability needed for design impact analysis.

Tool support is necessary but not sufficient. You need to take traceability into consideration when designing Decision Services and when implementing associated business rule repositories and business rules management environments. Build these systems with the need to trace the impact of change on your design in mind.

A similar approach can be used to see how information elements that change might impact the Decision Service. From an Input Data it should be possible to list all the Decisions and thus business rules that use that data. From an attribute or information item it should be possible to see all the business rules that use it in either their conditions or consequences. Any features derived from these attributes can be determined and this leads to the machine learning or analytic models that use those features. This trace information can be essential when an attribute's allowed values change or when some other element of the information model must be altered. Even when the change is a change to the distribution or range of values in an attribute, it will be important to evaluate each business rule and predictive analytic model that uses the attribute. Expected changes in the data values can be just as disruptive as changes to the structure of the data. For instance, a rule might be intended to identify which customers are top customers and the company might expect to have 10% of customers in this group. If the distribution of values in the data changes, the same rule might start identifying significantly more than 10% of customers as "top" customers, and this could be very expensive and disruptive. When data elements change either structurally or in terms of the distribution of values, it is common for every impacted decision to need to be changed.

> **Impact analysis is recursive**
>
> Design impact analysis often needs to be recursive. For instance, when a change in data affects a decision implemented as a predictive analytic model, it may be necessary to review all the business rules in decisions that require the results of the model to see if any of them must also change.

Improve Decision Effectiveness

The next step is to assess the overall performance of the Decision Service—is it making good decisions most of the time? This is true regardless of whether one approach is being used for all decisions or if several approaches are being tried for comparison. If the overall performance is unsatisfactory, then some change must be made to the current decision approach.

> **There is always value in monitoring decision effectiveness**
>
> It might seem that for a completely regulated or policy-driven decision that there is no value to assessing the effectiveness of a decision. After all, there is no flexibility to the decision-making. In reality, most Decision Services have some flexibility—if not in how the decision is made, at least in which decisions are referred for manual review. A regulated decision may be assessed to see if the rate of referral is acceptable for instance.

Decision effectiveness is primarily assessed in terms of the impact of the decisions made on the business metrics and KPIs associated with the decision. If decisions are being made effectively, then the decisions will be making a positive contribution to the overall KPIs and metrics. Decision effectiveness can also be assessed in terms of the number of decisions that cannot be made—that must be referred for manual review. Time and cost to make a decision might also be relevant, especially when outside data sources are involved. It may sometimes be possible to make an auto underwriting decision without paying for a report from the Department of Motor Vehicles. Considering the average cost of making a decision would then be part of the decision effectiveness measurement, even if this cost was not a KPI (though it is likely to be).

Decision effectiveness can be assessed both in terms of current performance and in terms of likely performance if the decision-making approach is not changed. When performance shows a slow but steady decline, for instance, it may not be a question of making a change to correct for a current problem but to prevent a future problem. Similarly, if there is likely to be a change in consumer behavior, after an election or natural disaster for instance, then the effectiveness might be assessed in the light of that change.

Decision Service performance matters also

The time it takes for a Decision Service to make a decision also matters. This performance should be monitored and tracked over time to ensure that the Decision Service performs adequately for the business need. If the Decision Service is supporting a customer interaction, for instance, then the response time must reflect that. If the Decision Service must process every customer overnight in a batch then the expected growth in customers must not increase the size of the batch window beyond that available.

If the speed to decision for a Decision Service is not adequate or is trending to become inadequate then the design will need to be reviewed to see how performance can be improved, perhaps by re-writing business rules or re-evaluating predictive analytic models.

When the current or likely future performance is unsatisfactory, some analysis of the root causes is called for. It may be that the performance of the Decision Service is unsatisfactory across the board. What is more likely is that it is unsatisfactory for subsets of the decisions being made. For instance, a cross-sell decision may not be driving as many additional sales as intended. It may be that this cross-sell decision is just underperforming. What is more likely is that the way cross-sell offers are being selected means that some segments of the customer base are getting poorly judged offers—perhaps high net worth individuals are getting inappropriate offers. Drilling down into the decision performance to find out exactly what is wrong is essential, if systematic improvement is to be undertaken. Similarly, if large numbers of decisions are being referred for manual review, it may be that this is always because a particular set of information is missing or inaccurate.

The end result of this analysis is an identification both of the kind of change that is called for and the subset(s) of decisions for which this change is appropriate. Several different changes may be required for a decision, for different segments of customers for instance.

Compare Multiple Approaches

If the current Decision Service has been implemented with multiple approaches, then any assessment of decision performance should include an assessment of the alternative approaches currently deployed. The approaches should be compared both at the macro level to see which results in the best overall results. They should also be compared at the micro level to see how the various approaches implemented work for different segments of the customers, partners or suppliers for which decisions are being made.

If the decision-making approaches have been implemented using an A/B testing mindset, then they should have been applied to the same number of transactions and the kinds of transactions should be similar between the two approaches. A simple comparison is therefore possible. If a champion-challenger approach has been used instead, then the number of transactions and the kinds of transactions passed into each decision-making approach will have to be considered. For instance, a champion might handle 95% of all transactions while a challenger only handles 5%. While the number of decisions made with the challenger should be high enough that the distribution and average result can be compared directly, it is possible that the challenger will have too few transactions in certain categories. For instance, if there is a very low rate of fraudulent transactions, then the number of fraudulent transactions handled by the challenger may be too small to be statistically significant.

As with the overall decision performance, the effectiveness of multiple approaches may not be consistently different. One approach may be more effective for a particular segment while the other is more effective in general. Understanding the details of the relative performance is critical to designing an appropriate new approach.

One of the most effective techniques for comparing two decision-making approaches is swapset analysis. In swapset analysis, the decisions made for a set of transactions are compared for a pair of decision-making approaches. Each transaction or customer is processed using one of the decision-making approaches, and the outcome recorded. Each is then processed using the second decision-making approach. Each transaction in the test set now has two results that can be compared—the result of running that transaction through the first decision-making approach and the result of running it through the second decision-making approach. A swapset analysis is a report with two axes, the vertical showing the possible outcomes from the first decision-making approach, and the horizontal from the second. Each cell of this report contains a number—the number of transactions that had the outcome from the first approach corresponding to the cell's horizontal position, and the outcome from the second approach corresponding to the cell's vertical position.

In the example shown in Figure 7-2, two different fraud detection approaches are being compared. Of the 10,000 test transactions, we can see that the first approach decided that 5,200 had the default response, 4,550 were fast tracked and 250 were referred for fraud investigation. When compared with the second approach we can see that 230 of those that previously got the default response were referred for fraud in the second approach while 45 of those referred for fraud under the first approach were not so referred with the second approach. Overall the second approach showed an increased in fraud referrals from 250 to 435.

			APPROACH 2		
		Total	Standard	Fast Track	Fraud
APPROACH 1	Standard	5,200	4,970		230
	Fast Track	4,550		4,550	
	Fraud	250	45		205
	Total	10,000	5,015	4,550	435

Figure 7-2 A swapset analysis report

This might be what was expected or it might not, and the swapset

163

analysis gives both an easy-to-use overview of the difference between the two approaches and the ability to drill down into those transactions referred for fraud in the first approach but not the second.

In addition, you should use the performance reporting tools developed to assess the effectiveness of approaches both at an overall level and in terms of specific subsets of transactions or customer segments.

Refreshing Models and Algorithms

When a predictive analytic model has been deployed into a Decision Service, it is based on the data available when it was developed. Over time the available data changes. These changes need to be reflected in a refreshed model. Such a refresh takes the new data and uses it to tune or update the model to make more accurate predictions given the changing circumstances. This refresh should occur at regular intervals as new data is collected.

> **Always have a plan to refresh predictive analytic models**
>
> One of the worst mistakes an organization can make when adopting predictive analytic models or machine learning algorithms is to have no process or plan for refreshing the models it is using. All models degrade over time, and some manual or automatic process is essential for any model that will remain in production beyond a single point in time.

Predictive analytic models can be refreshed manually by the modeling team that originally created them. Such a refresh is quicker than the original construction but still requires some manual effort. An automatic model refresh process can be established. The effect is like self-learning models, though the deployed model was initially created by an analyst and usually starts from a position of strong performance. As new data is collected, the model is automatically re-built using this new data and then automatically deployed. The new model either offers improved accuracy or corrects for declining accuracy in the face of changing circumstances. This technique usually works best when the predictive model is an ensemble of multiple predictive analytic models where the final output is being delivered using voting techniques across all the models.

164

Self-Learning Models

Machine learning can be used to create a self-learning predictive analytic model that is automatically re-built and updated as new data is collected. This approach is good for situations where there are limited analytic skills within an organization, when the situation changes rapidly (making manual assessment of model effectiveness impractical), and when models only need to be "good enough"—such as when delivering banner advertisements on a website.

Self-learning models can be established to create continuous online learning environments. These can avoid making the same mistake twice, essentially "rewriting" the decision-making approach as data is collected on its effectiveness.

When model transparency is critically important or when models must be explicable, such as in regulated industries like consumer credit, self-learning models are less appropriate.

Self-learning approaches can also be useful for new situations where no historical data has yet been gathered. The initial recommendations made based on self-learning approaches are, by the very nature of this approach, somewhat random and therefore may not be appropriate. They will, however, rapidly improve as the model learns.

Develop New Approach

There are a number of possible ways to design new or changed decision-making approaches. If multiple approaches are already in use, then it is possible that one of these approaches, or some combination of several, is the right approach to use going forward. Alternatively, a completely new approach may be called for, and this might involve also creating new challengers. Optimization might be able to find new approaches that improve results.

Use Existing Approaches

In Decision Services where multiple approaches were being executed – A/B or Champion/Challenger testing was integrated – several possible design approaches can be taken:

- **Promote challenger**: If you have been running multiple challenger approaches, it is possible that one of the challenger approaches will clearly outperform both the champion and all the other challengers. If you have such a challenger, and you are sure it outperforms in every segment, then this can be "promoted" to become your new champion approach. Simply use the rules and analytic models that describe the challenger strategy to replace the existing champion's rules and models.

- **Select from A/B approaches**: If you have been doing A/B testing, then it is similarly possible that one of the approaches will be clearly more effective than its peers. In general with A/B testing, you update the decision-making approach to use the most effective approach for all transactions for a period of time—the A/B test period will come to an end and a new standard approach will be implemented.

- **Synthesize a new approach**: Often you will find that a challenger will outperform the champion in some segments but not others, or that several challengers outperform the champion in different ways. You may find that several approaches in the A/B test have potential. In these circumstances you will synthesize a new approach by combining the effective elements of the various approaches into a new champion or standard approach.

- **Design a wholly new approach**: If your results have been poor, or if a major change to your environment has occurred, you may need to define a wholly new approach. In this situation, it will be important to conduct the maximum amount of design time analysis and simulation, as you will have little or no real effectiveness data on which to base your design.

- **Build new challengers**: One last step is to create new challenger strategies. Regardless of whether the current champion outperformed your challengers or whether you had a successful challenger or challenger(s), you will likely retire the unsuccessful challengers. To continue experimenting, you will need to design new challengers with different characteristics.

Determine if Multiple New Approaches Are Required

Any decision in the Decision Service may have been designed initially with a single decision-making approach. Such a decision will have a single coherent set of decisions on which it depends. When determining the best way to improve this decision, it may be apparent that several distinct approaches could be tried. As with the original design, either A/B or Champion/Challenger testing can be used to see which of these approaches is to be preferred moving forward.

If there is no particular reason to believe that one of the possible approaches will be better than the others, then an A/B testing approach can be applied. As previously noted, in this approach several equally good approaches are designed and transactions are distributed evenly between them. The decision-making approaches implemented will generally make different assumptions about what will work.

When the current approach has a long and successful history, there will be strong pressure not to change it. Defining a champion-challenger approach to this decision is required where most transactions will continue to run through the established or *champion* approach. A small percentage of all transactions are not handled with the current decision-making approach. Instead they are processed using one of potentially several *challenger* decision-making approaches. Because each challenger only handles a small number of transactions, this approach minimizes the risk of trying something radically different while still gathering the data necessary to see if that radical approach is worth trying.

Whether A/B or Champion/Challenger testing is adopted, the decision model will need to be refined to include multiple approaches as described earlier. In addition, the implementation of the Decision Service will need to allocate transactions correctly between the approaches and track which ones was used for each. Often it is useful and practical to execute all the approaches defined for the decision and store them for analysis – the Decision Service runs all the necessary calculations and logic but then only proceeds with one of them. This will create a richer dataset for later analysis.

Using Optimization to Refine Decision-making Approaches

Besides its use during decision-making, optimization technology can be used to analyze historical results to improve future decision-making. Two main scenarios exist—using optimization to prepare optimized actions for future decisions and using optimization to improve the business rules in a decision.

Once you have data about how a decision is being made you can analyze how those decisions worked out in business terms. Using machine learning to create predictive analytic models, you can see what is likely to happen and what the behavior of customers is likely to be in response to specific actions. This information can be used in an optimization model to determine the optimal action to be taken in specific scenarios. For instance, an optimization model could determine that if a customer in a certain segment walks into a branch or contacts the call center then the best action is to try and up-sell a specific credit product. The optimization model applied constraints like the total amount of credit risk we are prepared to tolerate, managed the tradeoffs of making this offer rather than another one, and considered the value of using our available pool of credit for this offer rather than for something else. These optimal actions then become input to the decision-making of a Decision Service.

Turning optimal actions into business rules

Assigning optimal actions in this way works well for fixed sets of known customers. What it does not always do is suggest an optimal action for an unknown, new customer. One way to resolve this is to add the optimal action to the customer data set you have and then apply a decision tree building or other machine learning algorithm to this data. You can then mathematically build a decision tree that predicts who will get which action—a set of customer characteristics selects a branch in the tree that assigns a specific action to the customer.

Such a decision tree can then be deployed as discussed in chapter 6 for execution in a Decision Service. Now, instead of explicitly linking an action to a specific customer, the optimization links a set of customer characteristics to an action using the decision tree. This can be applied to existing customers or to new ones—even to anonymous web visitors. This approach also handles the situation where critical customer data changes between the execution of the optimization and the assignment of the action. For instance, if a customer deposits a bonus check and then calls the call center their savings balance may be much higher than when the optimization was performed. The action assigned at the time may therefore be less accurate than the one that the decision tree assigned to people with higher balances.

In a Decision Service, policies and regulations often dictate eligibility at a fairly coarse-grained level. For example, a mortgage product might require a credit risk score of at least 800 while a Gold loyalty card might require at least $3,000 of purchases in a year. Optimization could be used to manage these thresholds at a more granular level. An optimization model could also decide that the optimal score threshold for a particular customer segment, those existing customers with good history who live in the Northeast, should be 723 while it should be 745 for a similar customer living in the South. The optimization model considers all the constraints and tradeoffs to maximize the value of your decision-making by setting appropriate thresholds and values in your business rules. This analysis can be repeated periodically using new data collected to keep the business rules in your decisions tuned.

In both scenarios optimization technology works offline—outside the Decision Service—and allows you to do what-if analysis. You can define various around risk/growth/profit scenarios, make an informed set of high-level decisions and then let the optimization work out the details. For instance, if you think you can take on another 2-3% in operational risk, then you can use optimization to see what the impact of this would be. The optimization model will optimally allocate that additional risk, probably by allocating more credit to customers with lower scores, and will ensure you get the greatest return for your additional risk.

Optimization is not always needed

Optimization is not needed in every Decision Service. In a significant minority of them, however, the use of optimization adds real value. Optimization can boost business performance by a few crucial percentage points creating value that goes straight to the bottom line.

Implement New Decision-Making Approaches

Once the appropriate response to a change in the environment or to current decision performance has been determined, it must be developed. New business rules, new predictive analytic models, and new optimization models must be designed and developed to implement the new decision-making approach(es) required.

Much of the design and development required is the same as the original steps in developing the decision-making approach for a new Decision Service, described in Chapter 5. Because there is an existing Decision Service there are, however, a few differences. Business rules may be managed and changed using a business rules management environment specifically intended for ongoing changes. Predictive analytic models may need to be re-built from scratch, but they are more likely to need to be re-calibrated and updated. If multiple decision-making approaches are in use already, then these may form the basis for a new approach; if multiple approaches are going to be developed for deployment, then these will need to be compared both to existing approaches and to each other before being finalized.

Confirm the Impact Is as Expected

Before deploying any new decision-making approach, it is important to be sure that it will behave as expected. This may not be 100% possible. The responses of customers to new decision-making approaches cannot be completely modeled in advance, for instance. Nevertheless, the most rigorous approach possible should be applied. The impact of a new decision-making approach should always be considered in terms of its *business* impact. The IT department will need to do testing to ensure stability, performance, connectivity, etc. This is no different than it would be for any other change to a production application. Without an ability to do business impact analysis, however, the full value of systematic decision monitoring and improvement cannot be delivered.

This impact analysis can and should be performed at various stages throughout the creation of new decision-making approaches. Wherever possible, it should be led by the business users with support from the IT and analytics teams as necessary—it is business impact that must be assessed, after all. The analysis should:

- Verify that the authors of the new decision-making approach have entered the business rules and predictive analytic models accurately and that the results are as expected, or at least well understood.

- Make an assessment on the overall impact the new decision-making approach will have once it is deployed into business operations.

Four main approaches can be used to assess the business impact— testing, simulation, what-if analysis, and advanced simulation. In most cases, the decision-making approach can be assessed using tools within the design environment, but sometimes it must be made available as a Decision Service outside the production environment.

Testing

In simple cases (for example, where a decision is based on a series of straightforward rules), it may be possible to validate that the decision-making approach will perform as expected simply by testing individual records (or a sample of individual records) and verifying that the Decision Service returns the expected answer (e.g. No Gold Customers get automatically referred for Fraud Investigation). This could involve scoring a sample of real (historical) data against the Decision Service, or it can sometimes be helpful to configure a data set that is specially generated to give a cross section of cases with known data permutations—true "test cases." This is especially useful when you want to test that certain rare, but important, situations will be correctly handled.

Simulation

Although useful for verification, individual record tests don't give any feel for what will happen over a period of time, or for a specific group of cases as a whole. For this, an aggregated rather than an individual level analysis is required, usually referred to as Simulation. The new decision-making approach should be executed against large sets of real or at least realistic data. For example, a standard set of example claims may be used for an initial simulation and then a more detailed simulation run against all claims in the last 60 days. The results of using the new decision-making approach are then compared with using the previous one on the same data.

Although simulations can identify unexpected or undesirable outcomes, they don't necessarily identify whether the issue lies with user error (incorrect application of the business rules or models), or whether the result is actually an accurate representation of the Decision Service. Testing may well help with the former situation, but the latter situation can be more difficult to deal with, perhaps requiring a more strategic choice to be made as to whether the business is willing to accept the unexpected outcome. If it is not, then the Decision Service may need to be adjusted until the simulation produces a suitable outcome.

What-if Analysis

What-if analysis is really an extension of simulation, providing the same aggregate level information. In addition, it allows the user to compare the outcomes of the Decision Service when certain parameters are adjusted. The goal might be to refine the Decision Service so that it makes more sense in the context of the business situation, maybe at the cost of the overall business value. For example, the optimal solution may be to refer 10% of cases to the Fraud Investigation Unit for investigation, but if the unit only has resources sufficient to assess 5%, then the Decision Service must be adjusted to make sure it doesn't refer more than 5% of cases. Alternatively, the business expert may wish to assess and compare scenarios where certain business values are varied (available budget, costs and revenues, for example). Through this kind of what-if analysis, the user may be able to identify a Decision Service that generates more revenue without necessarily decreasing overall purchase rates, for example. Another common reason would be to identify how the Decision Service functions across different points of interaction such as the web, mobile and call center channels

Advanced Simulation

The importance of good sample data to simulate on cannot be underestimated. Unfortunately, it is not always easy to obtain. Sometimes there will be no historical data available—perhaps this is a new Decision Service that hasn't been implemented before. In other cases, the situation being simulated could be so variable that no single sample of data will be sufficient. This is where advanced techniques like Monte Carlo simulation can become useful.

Don't use samples

It is increasingly unacceptable, and unnecessary, to use sample data for simulation and impact analysis. Modern tools and data infrastructure, high performance hardware and the cloud all combine to make it practical to use all your data. Building your simulation environment to use all your data – all of last year's claims, say – will create more confidence in the results.

These techniques can be used to generate the analysis based on less well-defined distributions of values in place of known data points that the user specifies based on their knowledge of the situation. As with a normal simulation analysis, the results will give an indication of the behavior of the Decision Service once it is deployed, but in addition, there will be some indication of how reliable the simulation result is.

Deploy the Change

Once the new decision-making approaches have been developed and evaluated to ensure that the business outcome is as expected, they must be deployed. For most changes, this involves using the same approaches used originally to define the Decision Service. New business rules and new predictive analytic or optimization models are deployed to replace existing ones. Others are deployed alongside existing ones for champion-challenger or A/B testing.

This deployment may seem just like any other IT update for a production system. At some level this is even true. With Decision Services, however, the number of updates is going to be dramatically higher. Some Decision Services are updated every day, with hundreds of pricing rules being changed for instance. Others have regular updates every week or every month. Existing IT processes and approaches may not scale to support this pace of change.

Complement existing IT processes

It is generally not possible or desirable to change the IT processes concerned. Instead, develop a new set of processes specifically for deploying and managing changes to Decision Services. A business rule development lifecycle that coordinates with the existing software development lifecycle but is optimized for business rules will work better than force fitting business rules into the existing approach. For instance, a change requiring only new business rules to be deployed should be simple and involve little IT coordination while a change that involves both rules and new data requirements will require coordinated changes.

---

8. Conclusion

Digital Decisioning delivers an exciting class of information systems. Organizations have been implementing Digital Decisioning for long enough to prove how well it works. Digital decisioning has helped many organizations reach new levels of business performance and delivered always-on, customer-centric systems that maximize operational effectiveness. These organizations could not operate at the level they do without these systems.

Yet many organizations lack Digital Decisioning. Their systems remain hard to change and manage, with business people and IT teams on opposite sides of an ongoing argument. Analytics and machine learning are kept separate from operational systems, limiting the ability of the analytic or data science team to apply their insights in day-to-day activities. Artificial intelligence is regarded as a separate technology stack from core operational systems. And systems don't learn, so they continue to behave the way they have always behaved even as markets, consumers, and competitors change around them.

The opportunity for these organizations is clear. They can develop analytic, adaptive and agile systems and deliver the promise of Digital Decisioning. They can change their organizations for the better. They don't need to wait for technology to come out of a research lab somewhere or adopt "bleeding edge" systems. The technology they need is proven, mature, and robust.

Digital decisioning is a powerful tool for enhancing existing business processes and legacy systems. Often requiring only minor changes to existing infrastructure, it can add value to what you already have. Bringing together business, IT, and analytic professionals around a common purpose, Digital Decisioning will change how your organizations see their information systems. Focusing on the four principles – keeping the decision in mind; being transparent and agile, becoming predictive rather than reactive; and committing to test, learn, and continuously improve - is the key.

Building these systems is a well understood and defined process that has just three steps:

- First, you must discover and model the decisions that you

will automate. The repeatable operational decisions that drive day-to-day behavior are the decisions that matter here. Understanding, describing, and modeling these decisions is the foundation for Digital Decisioning.

- Next, you can design and implement these decisions as Decision Services. Easy to integrate, manage, and change, Decision Services are a new class of service. Each Decision Service brings together the right combination of business rules, predictive analytics, machine learning, artificial intelligence and optimization technology to deliver accurate, repeatable decisions.

- Finally, you create the processes and infrastructure to continually monitor and improve the way your decisions are made. Responding to changing circumstances, challenging existing approaches to find better ones, and experimenting with new data all help ensure that your decisions are always as effective as possible.

Adopting this approach is an ongoing process. Because there are always more decisions to find and automate you must keep looking for new opportunities. Changing business conditions, new opportunities and evolving attitudes to automation all mean that your decision inventory will grow. Because decisions keep changing, your existing inventory must be monitored and improved constantly. This is not a one-time effort but a permanent change in how you think about information systems.

One final piece of advice: Don't wait. Your organization can benefit from Digital Decisioning today. Digital Decisioning can be developed and integrated quickly into your existing systems and processes. It can make the systems you have, the people you have, smarter and it can do so now.

The final chapter is a set of enablers for digital decisioning. A series of people, process and technology enablers are summarized with links to longer online versions, often with links for additional reading.

9. Bibliography

Decision Management
Taylor James (2011). *Decision Management Systems*. IBM Press.
Taylor James & Raden, Neil (2007). *Smart (Enough) Systems*. Prentice Hall.

Decision Modeling
Taylor James & Purchase, Jan (20170. *Real-World Decision Modeling with DMN*. MK Press
Debvoise Tom & Taylor, James (2014). *Microguide to Process and Decision Modelling in BPMN/DMN*. Advanced Component Research.
Fish, Alan (2012). *Knowledge Automation*. John Wiley and Sons.
Silver, Bruce (2016). *DMN Method and Style*. Cody-Cassidy Press.
von Halle Barbara & Goldberg, Larry (2010). *The Decision Model*. CRC Press.

Business Rules
Boyer Jérôme and Hafedh, Mili (1998). *Agile Business Rule Development*. Springer.

Machine Learning
Abbott, Dean (2014). *Applied Predictive Analytics*. John Wiley and Sons.
Berry, Michael & Linoff, Gordon (2011). *Data Mining Techniques*. Wiley Publishing, Inc.
Davenport, Tom (2018). *The AI Advantage*. MIT Press.
Davenport, Tom, & Harris, Jeanne (2007). *Competing on Analytics*. Harvard Business School Press.
Davenport, Tom, Harris, Jeanne, & Morison, Robert (2010). *Analytics at Work*. Harvard Business Press.
Provost, Foster & Fawcett, Tom (2013). *Data Science for Business*. O'Reily Media.
Siegel, Eric (2016). Predictive Analytics. John Wiley and Sons.

Optimization
Rossi, Francesca, van Beek, Peter, & Walsh, Toby (2006). *Handbook of Constraint Programming*. Elsevier Science.
Sashihara, Steve (2011). *The Optimization Edge*. McGraw-Hill.

Business or Other

Ayres, Ian (2007). *Super Crunchers*. Bantam Books.

Bossidy, Larry, & Charan, Ram (2002). *Execution*. Crown Business.

Fisher, Ronald A (1971). *The Design of Experiments*. Macmillan.

Osinga, Frans P.B (2007). *Science Strategy and War*. Routledge, 2007.

Pfeffer, Jeffrey, & Sutton, Robert (2006). *Hard facts, dangerous half-truths, and total nonsense*. Harvard Business School Publishing.

Pfeffer, Jeffrey, & Sutton, Robert (2000). *The Knowing-Doing Gap*. Harvard Business School Publishing,

10. Enablers for Success

The previous chapters walked through the key steps in implementing Digital Decisioning. They showed how to discover and model the decisions that should be implemented. They described the design and implementation of Decision Services, the core of Digital Decisioning. And they discussed the importance of monitoring and systematically improving decisions over time and how to go about that.

There are some critical enablers for success in Digital Decisioning. These enablers have been grouped into the three following sections:

- People Enablers
- Process Enablers
- Technology Enablers

These enablers can be thought of as tips and asides that were too long to be embedded as notes within the main text. Each enabler stands largely alone, and there is no particular reason they appear in the order they do. You can dip in and out of this chapter as you like when and if the enablers seem helpful in your journey. Each enabler is summarized here, but more information is available online.

People Enablers

Digital Decisioning is about optimizing decision-making to fuel the most beneficial business results. This means it can't just be about technology, it has to involve people. Digital Decisioning requires both the right technologies and the collaboration between business people, the IT department, and analytic or data science teams. These organizations will all have to deal with change, too. And once you have success, scaling it requires a center of excellence to drive broad and deep adoption.

The Three-Legged Stool

To ensure a strong "three-legged stool," it's critical to encourage three-way conversations among business, analytic, and IT groups and to start building collaborative skills. These types of activities will foster teamwork and will help all groups acquire a more holistic and all-encompassing perspective as they work together toward more effective and informed Digital Decisioning:

- Get the teams together for project meetings that align with Digital Decisioning objectives and methodologies.

- Provide cross-training to enable each team to gain an understanding of the other teams' terminology, technologies, and overall approach.

- Invite all teams to train on new enabling technologies so they can gain insights on how they can make the most of them.

- Host lunch-and-learn sessions so that members of each team can do a deeper dive and share their expertise with the other groups.

In Digital Decisioning projects, decision discovery is key and should be done early in the process. There are a lot of good reasons for this:

- It sets the stage for future activities and ensures inclusivity.

- Having upper management of all three groups work together ensures that Digital Decisioning initiatives map to business processes, create a shared sense of direction, and build lasting relationships and a culture of cooperation.

https://bit.ly/ddbook01

- Engaging analytics teams at this stage can help build predictability models and guide business and IT decision-making in a more measured and analytic way.

- Mapping the expertise all three groups have to offer and ensuring that information is supported with reliable, verifiable data keeps the model grounded and involves all three groups.

By aligning personal objectives with business results, each group will be motivated to focus their efforts on the end result: to help drive the best possible decisions during the digital transformation process.

Dealing With Organizational Change

Like any change, implementing Digital Decisioning can be disruptive to organizations and engender resistance, even if the result will ultimately be positive. It's a natural response because people have a comfort level with the status quo. Knowledge workers may find that the nature of their work has changed. Supervisors may feel that they are losing control because the system is managing approvals. IT may lack confidence in the stability of new systems needed to support business requirements. And even customers may notice changes in the way they engage with the organization.

Understanding how change is perceived across the organization will help you better manage expectations and emotional responses. A positive response to change will likely evoke enthusiasm at first, followed by informed pessimism, as stakeholders start to grasp what it involves, such as additional training, changes in procedures, and potential risk to bonuses. In time, people will come around to an attitude of informed optimism and will embrace change.

Negatively perceived change has a different dynamic. The "Kubler-Ross grief cycle" is a metaphor to describe how people respond to traumatic events, and it can be applied to the cultural response in an organization undergoing digital transformation. For example, for people who work day in and day out in a call center, adapting to a new system may seem traumatic. Common emotional responses to change that is perceived negatively may include immobilization, denial, anger, and depression. As people move through these stages, bargaining comes into play, and when that fails to change anything, they will gradually move toward acceptance.

https://bit.ly/ddbook02

In any case, it's important to manage change over time and to understand that certain changes may take longer than others in order to gain acceptance.

A Digital Decisioning Center of Excellence

A Center of Excellence, or CoE, is essential for long term success in Digital Decisioning. Because Digital Decisioning requires the coordination of multiple disciplines and areas of expertise across the entire organization, a central focal point for learning and sharing ideas is crucial. When designing a CoE, start by establishing the organizational structure, determining staffing needs, defining processes, and articulating its mission. An effective CoE will create a strong foundation for expanding your adoption of Digital Decisioning.

Every organization and every digital transformation initiative is different—there is no one-size-fits-all CoE. You can also expect your CoE to evolve and change over time, so it's important to establish both short-term and long-term

objectives and guidelines. Initially, you may need to focus on getting early adopters up to speed in order to accelerate the success of your first Digital Decisioning initiatives. Later on, you may want to focus on monitoring actual projects to ensure consistency, optimal use of existing assets, and best practices.

The CoE is often responsible for leading and managing return on investment, or ROI, for a Digital Decisioning project. The data that is collected, analyzed, and reported at each juncture needs to be accurate and honest and not manipulated to make people look good. All this is essential in order to get a true picture of the improvements resulting from digital transformation and to demonstrate a positive impact on the bottom line.

Process Enablers

Putting thought, effort, and resources into developing the right processes to support Digital Decisioning is essential to driving it forward and achieving broad adoption across your organization. There are a number of different facets to this undertaking. A process for maintaining your decision inventory and a new software development lifecycle are two such key processes. Additionally, integrating Decision Services and business processes, encouraging a culture of experimentation and fact-based decision making, and implementing the Observe-Orient-Decide-Act (OODA) loop can help establish best practices and methodologies.

Managing A Decision Inventory

The foundation of a successful Digital Decisioning program is an up-to-date, accurate, and well-managed decision inventory built collaboratively by business stakeholders, IT, and analytic groups. The benefit of this inventory is that it helps everyone involved understand decisions and their dependencies in your business, especially the repeatable ones. A model of decisions and their dependencies, as well as their relationship with your performance management and business process environments, gives you a solid foundation for developing Digital Decisioning systems.

Some organizations favor a single effort for the entire organization. While this approach may work for an organization, there are some problems with it. It is challenging to show the business value. Plus, failure rates for these kinds of projects are often high.

The best approach is to build out and manage a decision inventory, business process by business process. The inventory should be dynamic and managed over time. As new data is gathered and introduced, it should be continually factored in and synchronized with performance management changes. And to really ensure the effectiveness of your decision inventory, it needs to be linked to the implementation components you develop along the way.

Like decision discovery, a decision inventory requires active collaboration across business, IT, and analytic teams and a COE—regardless of who ultimately takes ownership. Different divisions and departments of your organization also need to be engaged, as decisions made by one group typically impact other groups. Ensuring that all relevant groups are involved will help improve the quality of Digital Decisioning and make it easier to develop more decisioning solutions over a period of time.

Perhaps one of the most important aspects of your decision inventory is how it links to specific key performance indicators (KPIs) and metrics. This helps the team evaluate whether decisions are good or bad and helps drive prioritization and design decisions in Digital Decisioning projects.

Adapting the Software Development Lifecycle

A key role for IT in the development of Decision Services is to capture the decision logic involved The focus of the IT Software Development Lifecycle (SDLC) therefore will be on capturing, designing, and implementing these business rules. Since the technology you'll be using to support the implementation of the Decision Service provides features that enable quick implementation of decisions and business rules, it's advisable to use an agile, incremental, and iterative approach as early as possible in the development cycle. It's

often challenging to define all the business rules supporting a decision up front, so an agile and iterative approach is the best path to success, as opposed to a rigid plan that is typical of traditional software development lifecycles.

Using the basic framework of a traditional implementation—discovery, development, and acceptance—an agile approach has multiple iterations underlying each of these three phases, and each iteration contains multiple loops or cycles. Development activities are grouped into cycles, so the Decision Service is built iteration by iteration, with the scope changing and growing over time. Each cycle includes activities like discovery workshops, analysis, prototyping, implementation, and testing tasks. Feedback is then consolidated at the end of each cycle. Business users are deeply involved in this process and collaborate closely with the development team, continually identifying new rules and providing them with new ideas for refining existing rules.

Decision Services also involve developing predictive analytic models using machine learning algorithms to improve the accuracy of decision-making through data analysis. A well-established approach for analytic development is the CRoss Industry Standard Process for Data Mining (CRISP-DM) (see below). While this is now somewhat dated, it still provides the best framework for analytic and machine learning development. Organizations that do not have a development lifecycle for analytics should adopt CRISP-DM and integrate it with their SDLC, especially the SDLC they adopt for business rule and Decision Service development.

A Culture of Experimentation

Experimentation is foundational to developing a Digital Decisioning program. It's especially helpful for operational or small-scale decisions having to do with transactions or managing customer relations and behaviors. Often, neither business people nor IT are comfortable with experimentation. IT is typically intent on finding the "right" answers—technical solutions that solve problems. And businesspeople believe in treating customers in the best possible way and are leery of alternative approaches. In any case, both groups need to learn that Digital Decisioning systems are iterative systems and are based on trying different approaches and learning from those experiences.

Operational decisioning and experimentation work hand in hand because you can run each experiment multiple times, because you can improve your decision-making approach continually and apply it to future decisions and because they generate the data you need to compare experimental approaches. Also, if your organization doesn't have adequate data to delineate an effective decision-making approach, operational decision experiments can create the data you need.

Apart from getting buy-in from IT and business units, it's also important to have a control group of customers, partners, or suppliers with whom the business engages by following the old approach, while the remainder of the population is engaged with following the new approach. This way, you can make a proper comparison as to which approach works better.

https://bit.ly/ddbook06

Finally, it's important to design your experiments so that you can review your results and draw conclusions that will ultimately guide your decision making. Ronald Fisher's book *The Design of Experiments*, first published in 1935 (Fisher, 1935), provides excellent guidance on the classical elements that go into experimental design, such as comparison, randomization, factorial considerations (where multiple factors and multiple combinations of these factors are tested), and others.

Moving to Fact-Based Decisioning

Long-term success with Digital Decisioning usually requires some cultural shifts. Creating a culture that embraces and values fact-based decisioning—which includes statistical awareness and presents data and decisions as a set—is paramount. But what if your stakeholders uphold intuition and experience over data and are resistant to fact-based

decisioning? What if they don't have statistical awareness or have a tendency to mistake correlation for causation? How do you gain acceptance for this approach if it's not aligned with your current corporate culture? These are all questions to ask yourself as you make this important cultural shift.

Here are few ideas to get you moving into a culture of fact-based decisioning:

- Build decision support systems that clearly spell out the decisions they support and present data in that context.
- Try to communicate to stakeholders that fact-based decisioning builds on a data strategy foundation complemented by expertise, so they understand that experience and intuition are considered valid and do figure into the equation.
- Use predictive analytic models to simplify large volumes of data to direct decision making toward what truly matters.
- Build a comprehensive information strategy.

The OODA Loop

Each time a business process or transaction executes, an operational decision is made. Tactical decisions are also made from time to time to hone operational decision criteria, allow for exceptions, and take corrective steps. But, over the long haul, these decisions are not enough to improve business outcomes. Business strategies also need to change to respond to new products that are introduced by the competition, consumer demand, and other aspects of the dynamic marketplace. All of these decisions—strategic, tactical, and operational—need to be aligned. And that is where the Observe, Orient, Decide, Act (OODA) loop comes into play.

Developed by US Army Colonel John Boyd, the OODA loop was originally applied to combat operations as a way of gaining the advantage by getting inside the opponent's thought process. The OODA loop is now used by non-military organizations to clarify the relationship between strategic and tactical decision, along with operational decisions—all of

which are important in Digital Decisioning.

Business outcomes are "observed" to detect changes. Based on these observations, new tactical decisions (such as improvements in business processes) are made during the "orient" and "decide" phases. In the "act" phase, operational decisions are made that follow the criteria set forth in the "decide" stage.

Let's break the OODA loop down into its key components:

- **Observe:** This step relates to measuring and understanding the performance of your Digital Decisioning in order to improve results over time. Rather than just observing results, it's even more useful—in an operational context—to assess and evaluate day-to-day decisions and ensure that they align with the strategy and tactics you are adopting.

- **Orient:** In order to be useful, these observations need to be interpreted. How we interpret the observations is colored by the culture, experience, and traditions of those who look at the data. Performance is also reviewed in the context of decisions that lead to the actions driving results.

- **Decide:** This part of the loop applies to choosing the appropriate decision-making approach (which may change from the original approach) based on observation and interpretation of the data.

- **Act:** Here's where you run the Decision Service and take action. Decision Services generate data that is fed back into the OODA loop on decisions made, choices that drove decisions, actions taken, and the results of the actions.

CRISP-DM and Digital Decisioning

Released in the year 2000, **CR**oss **I**ndustry **S**tandard **P**rocess for **D**ata **M**ining (CRISP-DM) is one of the most popular and effective frameworks for advanced analytics and data science projects. It is especially well suited for organizations that lack experience in these areas.

The CRISP-DM approach defines a business problem and gets an understanding of the available data. The data is prepared and analytically modeled until a result is achieved that can be evaluated and deployed. CRISP-DM is iterative and repeatable by design and consists of six phases:

- **Business understanding**: Determine business objectives and analytic goals and produce a project plan.
- **Data understanding**: Collect, describe, explore, and verify data quality.
- **Data preparation**: Select, clean, construct, integrate, and format data.
- **Modeling:** Select modeling technique(s), generate a test design, build the model, and assess it.
- **Evaluation:** Assess results and the process in order to determine next steps.
- **Deployment:** Plan the deployment, establish monitoring and maintenance processes, and finalize implementation.

https://bit.ly/ddbook09

When it comes to Digital Decisioning there are three aspects of CRISP-DM that play key roles: business understanding, business and IT engagement, and deploying and delivering business value.

Business Understanding

Before the analytical work begins, it's critical to have a firm grasp on the business objective and scenario. The goal is to develop models that assist with decision-making. Building decision models in the business-understanding phase helps clarify the business problem that analytics aim to solve, focuses on business decision-making not technical modeling, shows what role analytics play in decision-making and connects analytics to business objectives and processes.

Business and IT Engagement

An effective analytic model requires engagement of business and IT teams as well as data scientists. A decision model keeps everyone in the loop because the decision-making process is top of mind with each iteration. A decision model also allays the temptation to try out the latest "shiny object"—the coolest, newest approaches—and focuses instead on using the right tools for the project. For any new technology that the project team may be interested in trying out, they always need to ask themselves whether the new technology or data will help achieve stated business objectives.

Deploying and Delivering Business Value

Once a predictive analytic model is complete, it needs to be deployed so that the organization can extract value from it. Successful deployment involves coordinating the model with business rules and other analytic models into a Decision Service.

Decision models help strike a balance between machine learning and business rules, show how the business rules and predictive analytic models can work together, show what data is used when in decision-making and support monitoring machine learning performance by tracking how decisions are made and decision-making data to business outcomes.

Why Functional, Process and Data Approaches Don't Work

First and foremost, developing an effective Digital Decisioning system needs to start with the decision. Focusing on functions, process, or data does not work, and here is why:

- **Functional focus:** A traditional method of building systems is to focus on a cluster of related capabilities for one functional area and for a single functional department.

  This only works if the decisions are contained within a single business function, but not when decisions cut across multiple functional areas. A good example of this is a discount calculation decision, which usually requires inputs from many different functions, such as the supply chain, finance, and customer management.

  https://bit.ly/ddbook10

- **Process focus:** Some organizations have moved to end-to-end business processes that cut across and link multiple functional areas to create a desirable business outcome.

  This approach can help with identifying decisions but tends to intertwine decisions with the process itself. For true Digital Decisioning, business processes and decisions should be linked together but kept separate, so that the focus is always on the decisions.

- **Data focus:** When designing their own custom systems, some organizations may focus on the data that must be managed so

that it can be edited and displayed. Analysis is usually limited to reporting.

These systems can provide data for Decision Support systems but typically defer decision-making to actors outside the system.

Decision Characteristics

In the process of developing a Digital Decisioning system, it's important to gain an understanding of the key characteristics that define each decision. This information is essential when doing a decision inventory, as opposed to modeling a specific decision.

- **Volume:** The volume of a decision—how often it needs to be made in different contexts—constrains the level of automation involved in how a decision should behave. Volume also plays a role in determining human involvement.

- **Timeliness:** The more often a decision is made, the less time can be spent making the decision. At times, low-volume decisions, like responding to an emergency signal, can have short timeframes and need to occur instantly.

https://bit.ly/ddbook11

- **Consistency over time:** Some decisions remain consistent over time, while others are in a constant state of flux. For example, a decision may be made to update product pricing annually, as opposed to deciding on daily pricing adjustments based on the competitive landscape. Assessing the extent to which decisions will remain consistent over time will help you design an appropriate Digital Decisioning system.

- **Value range:** The difference between the value of the best possible decision and the impact of a bad one can vary tremendously. A small value range has less of impact on the business than a wide value range. The value range makes a big difference to the kind of Digital Decisioning system you build and the extent to which predictive analytics is part of the system.

- **Time to value:** The impact or value of some decisions is felt immediately, but, with others, that may take more time. When

the time to value is short, you get immediate feedback, which allows for rapid experimentation and adaptive Digital Decisioning. A decision with a long time to value needs to be monitored for an extended period. Experiments will have to be run over time so you can gather the data you need to evaluate the decision.

- **Degrees of freedom:** Some decisions are constrained by the policies and regulations that your organization must follow, whereas others have a greater degree of freedom. There may be some uncertainty in judging the success or failure of a decision. Judgment, analysis, and experimentation play a role in determining how these decisions should be made—now and in the future.

Prioritizing Decisions

Most business areas will have more decisions than can be addressed in a single Digital Decisioning project or set of projects. Decisions need to be prioritized so that incremental progress can be made. Understanding the most important success criteria and project goals will help you prioritize decisions more effectively. This will help you identify the metrics and KPIs that best align with the project's overall purpose. Below are some factors to look at in your prioritization process:

- How measurable is the decision's impact?
- How big is the difference between good and bad results in terms of revenue, risk, and loyalty?
- How often do you make the decision?
- How much spend is committed as a result of the decision?
- How much does it cost to make a decision?
- How difficult will it be to develop a Digital Decisioning project for a given decision?

The approach you take to prioritization depends on your organization's experience with Digital Decisioning and how open it is to change:

- If you are developing your first Digital Decisioning project, prioritize based on which decisions seem most readily

https://bit.ly/ddbook12

191

implemented and least controversial so that you can show early success.

- If you already have extensive portfolios of Digital Decisioning projects, look for opportunities to repurpose existing assets and infrastructure.

- If your organization struggles with organizational change, prioritize decisions that are already implemented in order to create less disruption, rather than replacing one automated decision with another.

Technology Enablers

The core technologies that form the foundation of Digital Decisioning systems typically include business rules management, machine learning, and optimization systems. You can choose to have your development team build these components from scratch, or you can use off-the-shelf systems. Pre-packaged systems for specific areas like insurance claims, loan approval, or marketing are available and can save you time and resources. Other key technologies that make up an effective Digital Decisioning system include data infrastructures and a service-oriented architecture that supports both a process- and event-centric development methodology.

Business Rules Management Systems

A Business rules management system (BRMS) is a complete set of software components for the creation, testing, management, deployment, and ongoing maintenance of business rules in a production operational environment. It is used by developers and other technical staff and by business users and analysts who can make routine changes and updates to the business rules that drive Decision Services. A BRMS uses common business terminology to define what will be manipulated by the rules and consists of these components:

- **Business rules repository:** Stores all the business rules and other components necessary to define a Decision Service and should support version control and maintain audit trails of

https://bit.ly/ddbook13

192

changes made.

- **Design tools:** Allow technical users to integrate business rules into the environment, including setting up data sources for the business rules to access, defining the data passed in and out of a Decision Service, and specifying additional integration parameters.

- **Rule maintenance interfaces:** Enable technical and non-technical users (like business analysts) to create and manage business rules.

- **Verification and validation tools:** Help a BRMS validate the completeness and correctness of business rules and should be available to both business and IT users.

- **Testing tools:** Tests business rules to confirm that outcomes are as expected. This component tests both standard cases and boundary conditions.

- **Business simulation tools:** Allows business and IT users to simulate the impact of proposed changes in business terms. Non-technical users need to see the impact a change would have on business metrics before they make the change. IT users can also make use of this functionality, but it must be focused on *business* impact, not technical execution.

- **Deployment tools:** Enable deployment of Decision Services on many different technical platforms and ensure that business rules are deployable on the designated platforms.

- **High-performance business rules engine:** Determines which rules need to be executed and in what order.

Machine Learning Platform

A Machine Learning Platform is a set of software components used to analyze data sources to determine mathematical relationships and develop a predictive analytic model based on those relationships. A machine learning platform is an important tool because it enables data scientists to perform some important tasks. These include connecting to data, preparing data for modeling, visualizing data, building predictive and statistical models, testing models, assessing the business impact of models, deploying models into production, and managing deployed models. A variety of modeling techniques are used to build models, each with its own application for decision-making.

Key components include:

- **A model repository**: A place where predictive analytic models and the specification of the tasks required to produce them are stored, revised, and managed.

https://bit.ly/ddbook14

- **Data management tools**: Used to enable machine learning algorithms to access multiple data sources of various formats.

- **Design tools for a modeler**: Help modelers define how data will be integrated, cleaned, and enhanced, as well as how it will be fed through machine learning algorithms and how the results will be analyzed and used.

- **Machine Learning algorithms**: Algorithms are applied to data in order to produce predictive analytic models.

- **Data visualization and analysis tools**: Help modelers understand data by analyzing distribution and other characteristics and by analyzing the results of a set of models in terms of their predictive power and validity.

- **Deployment tools**: Enable deployment of models as an API, as code, as SQL, as business rules, or to a database using an in-database analytics engine.

Optimization Systems

Mathematical optimization addresses a problem with a model based on your business objectives and constraints. The model is fed with actual data and produces optimized decisions. Optimization can be applied to a single transaction or to a set of transactions being traded off against each other.

https://bit.ly/ddbook15

Optimization can help you manage how you use shared or limited resources to drive your decision forward. You and your team create a model to solve a specific business problem by determining a set of actions. You can use mathematical optimization on a micro level for a single transaction, such as finding the right configuration of complex products to fit your customer's requirements. Or you can use it across multiple related micro-decisions that involve things like sharing limited resources, incurring costs wisely, or containing global risk. You can also use this technique to tune the thresholds or parameters of business rules in an existing Decision Service.

It consists of four software components:

- **Solver.** Uses a variety of mathematical approaches to find an optimal or best solution to a defined problem.

- **Modeling language.** Allows the effective specification of the variables, constraints and objective function of the optimization problem.

- **Design tools**. A set of tools to visualize the model, see results and analyze performance and to compare various approaches to optimization.

- **Interactive user interface**. Enables business analysts to create scenarios and adjust model parameters to compare solutions.

Pre-Configured Digital Decisioning Solutions

If you need to solve a specific, quantifiable business problem, you may want to consider using an out-of-the-box, pre-configured solution. These are often delivered as Software-as-a-Service (SaaS) solutions or as add-ons to existing applications, such as campaign management applications. The solutions consist of a combination of business rules, predictive analytic models, and/or optimization wrapped in a single application, so you can work from one easy-to-use interface.

These pre-configured systems are best for things like targeted direct marketing, inbound and outbound marketing, optimizing customer service, insurance and healthcare fraud, debt collection, price optimization, and more.

There are both pros and cons to using these solutions. The main advantages are simplicity (because the system is focused on just one business problem), a single user interface, lower IT requirements, SaaS options with lower overhead, easy-to-deploy updates, and pre-built content

https://bit.ly/ddbook16

195

(such as reports), and predefined rules. All of this saves an enormous amount of time. The downsides are less flexibility, few options for problems other than marketing or fraud issues, lack of integration with existing predictive analytics or business rules, and limited application beyond a specific problem.

Data Infrastructure

Data is foundational to Digital Decisioning. It's the basis for predictive analytic models and for analyzing the effectiveness of a given decision. Digital Decisioning must be integrated with your data infrastructure. This will ensure that the data required for a particular decision is passed to the system and recommended actions and associated information are returned.

These five data infrastructure components are frequently used with Digital Decisioning:

- **Operational databases:** These contain the transactional information needed at decision time and raw data for building predictive analytic models. Digital Decisioning needs quick access to live data for transactions being processed. Operational databases work well for this. Machine learning algorithms need history and transactional detail over time. Operational databases are not necessarily designed for this type of analytical work and additional data infrastructure may be required.

- **Data warehouses:** To complement operational databases, many organizations have data warehouses that are more integrated, better understood, and cleansed more thoroughly. A data warehouse can be configured to support the development of predictive analytic models, but some are not. If data warehouses are architected to store detailed transactional data and if cleansing and integration of data is handled at a transactional level, they can offer great value.

- **Analytic data marts:** These consist of data extracted from operational databases or from an enterprise data warehouse. Analytic data marts focus on a specific solution area and are owned by a single business unit. If structured properly, they

https://bit.ly/ddbook17

196

can be used to create predictive analytic models to support decisions in that business domain. Additionally, analytic data marts are well suited for performance analysis for a Digital Decisioning system.

- **In-database analytics:** Some vendors build machine learning into their databases. The big benefit is that the predictive analytic models can be built and scored without having to extract or move the data from the database. By accessing the data directly from the same server, performance is positively impacted.

- **Big Data platforms**: Data in such platforms is generally not as structured as data found in relational databases. It can be "semi-structured" (log data from applications, data from sensors or devices, or data from network traffic or operations) or "unstructured" (text documents, audio, and video). Newer machine learning algorithms are effective at turning this less structured data into analytical insight and predictive analytic models.

A Service-Oriented Platform

A Service-Oriented Architecture (SOA) consists of multiple coherent services that work together to deliver the total functionality required. Each service may be built in different languages or following different designs, but each element has an interface or protocol that allows other services to access it and collaborate with it.

- **SOA:** Digital Decisioning fundamentally relies on Decision Services, which answer decision-making questions for other services. These services can be deployed in any architectural framework, so an SOA is a great fit for Decision Services, as it allows for loosely coupled services that mesh easily with other services.

- **Business Process Management System (BPMS):** Defines and executes tasks involved in a business process such as data entry, integration of multiple systems, human tasks such as inspections or reviews, as well as automated tasks.

https://bit.ly/ddbook18

197

Digital Decisioning can automate decision-making involved in many of these tasks and can be used to determine which transactions need to be reviewed or need to be routed to specific users. The combination of BPMS and Digital Decisioning is often referred to as Intelligent Process Automation, IPA, or Intelligent BPMS, iBPMS.

- **Event Processing System:** Correlates events from any source over any time frame so that an appropriate action can be taken. Event Processing Systems determine what question to ask, and Digital Decisioning provides the answer. Streaming event data can be enriched with data at rest from a traditional data infrastructure.

Digital Decisioning Versus Decision Support

Digital Decisioning uses automation to make decisions based on a data set. Decision Support systems enable users to sift through data and perform analysis in order to help them make better decisions. Digital Decisioning differs from traditional Decision Support in five key ways:

https://bit.ly/ddbook19

1. Decision Support systems provide information that describes the situation and historical trends so that humans can decide which actions to take. Digital Decisioning automates or recommends the actions that should be taken based on the data available at the time the decision is made.

2. The policies, regulations, and best practices that determine the best action are generally embedded in Digital Decisioning. In a Decision Support system, it's up to users to incorporate them in their decision-making process.

3. Decision Support systems are generally reactive, in that human decision-makers react to a new or changed situation by accessing information that might help them make a decision. Digital Decisioning, on the other hand, is proactive and uses data to make predictions.

4. With Decision Support systems, users learn what works and what does not and apply their learning to future decisions. In

Digital Decisioning, experimentation, testing, and learning infrastructures are built in, so the *system* gets to know what works and what does not.

5. Decision Support systems are often desktop or interactive applications that are independent of core applications. Digital Decisioning, on the other hand, is tightly integrated into and make decisions for applications and services in the enterprise application architecture.

Best Practices for Decision Services Construction

There are several technical best practices worth considering when building a Decision Service:

- **Designing for batch and interactive:** Decisions can be made before the transaction occurs (example: pre-calculating the credit worthiness of known customers) or interactively while the transaction is in progress. Ideally, a Decision Service is designed once and deployed in a batch or interactive mode without recoding or changing the business rules, predictive analytic models, or optimization models.

  https://bit.ly/ddbook20

- **No side effects:** When designing a Decision Service, it is critical to avoid any "side effects." The Decision Service should be used solely for decision making and not for taking action (like sending emails or processing transactions). If the Decision Service were to take the action, then the service can only be called when that action is appropriate to the decision

- **Logging:** Decision Services should log how decisions were made, which business rules fired, the predictive scores calculated, what data was used, and what results were generated by optimization models. If a decision is regulated, it is critical to store these logs every time a decision is made so decisions can be traced. If a decision is not regulated, it is useful to log how decisions were made to help with the decision improvement process.

Iterative Development

An agile and iterative approach to building a Decision Service is preferable to building 100% of the functionality at once.

There are two paths to take:

- **The number of transactions handled by the Decision Service gradually increases.** This works well when the Decision Service makes a decision that would normally be made by a person. The initial version of the decision might handle relatively few transactions and leave the rest for manual review. These manual reviews help define, shape, and augment existing business rules. Business rules can then be compared to manual actions to see if the rules are getting closer to or even outperforming manual decision-making. Over a period of time, the number of rules and their sophistication can increase so that the Decision Service handles a larger percentage of transactions.

- **An automated decision is required.** The Decision Service that needs to deliver an appropriate ad to a web page cannot defer that kind of instantaneous decision to a person. The decision needs to be automated, but even this type of Decision Service can evolve over time. It might start out with a default response, which is to serve up a generic ad that can be used anytime. Then, when more rules and analytic models are added, the Decision Service can make more targeted responses in different circumstances and for different audiences.

www.ingramcontent.com/pod-product-compliance
Lightning Source LLC
Chambersburg PA
CBHW071213210326
41597CB00016B/1797